The Word and words

Beyond Gender in Theological and Liturgical Language

Women's Task Force
Worship Commission
of the
Consultation on Church Union

Edited by
William D. Watley

Published with the approval of the
Executive Committee

Copyright © 1983
Consultation on Church Union

ISBN 0-940186-03-9
The Word and words

Prices in USA and Canada
Single Copy — $3.00 plus postage

Copies available from
Consultation on Church Union
228 Alexander Street
Princeton, NJ 08540

TABLE OF CONTENTS

FOREWORD

When a journey is begun there is no way of anticipating all that will be encountered along the way. The goal can be clearly articulated but factors such as weather conditions on a trip, or independent variables in scientific experimentation, or the Holy Spirit in the life of the church, can lead us into new directions or open up to us new possibilities as we strive for the object of our quest.

When the Consultation on Church Union was born some twenty-one years ago, its goal of a uniting church was ascribed to by all. At that time certain issues, problems, and challenges were identified for resolution. However, during the course of its journey, the Consultation has been challenged and led to address itself to a number of other vital theological and ecclesiological concerns which work against the unity of the people of God and which are crucial to a church that seeks to be truly catholic and inclusive, truly evangelical, and truly reformed.

Issues such as racism, the concerns of the handicapped, and problems related to sexism, of which inclusive language is only one among many, can be viewed as challenges to the integrity and life of the Consultation. Or, these issues can be viewed as ways through which the Holy Spirit leads the church into becoming a truer existential embodiment of the Kingdom. The Consultation On Church Union adopts the latter view.

The Consultation is pleased to publish these presentations which were first given at our Language and Liturgy Convocation held at Scarritt College in Nashville, Tennessee, in November, 1981. The Consultation believes that the perspectives presented herein will add much to our journey in our efforts to live our way toward union and will make us more effective as proclaimers and livers of the Word/word.

William D. Watley
Princeton, New Jersey

January, 1983

INTRODUCTION

The consultation was undertaken at the initiative of the Women's Task Force, in cooperation with the Commission on Worship and the Executive Committee, as one contribution to the overcoming of the COCU identified "alert on sexism." Inclusive language with regard to human beings, but even more particularly inclusive language about God, continues to remind us of "church-dividing issues" which have emerged to thwart the "living of our way toward union." Since most all of our denominations are engaged in extensive study of this matter individually, it seemed appropriate for COCU to gather for mutual consultation those key leaders from the communions who are actively working on these problems (liturgists, feminists, theologians, curricula specialists, ecumenists, and selected pastors). This was the *first* time any such ecumenical endeavor had been called, and according to the individual evaluations received from participants, it was apparent that a significant event indeed had occurred through the Consultation on Church Union's sponsorship.

The goals of the consultation were as follows:

1. Exploring the theological implications of language about God and God's people in the scripture and liturgy;
2. Discovering the nature and function of living language in the development of theology;
3. Lifting up a vision of inclusiveness in the COCU quest;
4. Sharing of resources and specific tools developed by COCU;
5. Participating in various forms of inclusive worship;
6. Providing illustrations of the local church as an educational model for change.

On a scale of 1 (low) to 5 (high), 80% of the participants indicated that the goals had been met with either a "4" or a "5" ranking item. But more important, over 80% of the participants, when asked, "How important is inclusive language to Christian unity," checked "5," (almost all the others checked "4") indicating that the issue is absolutely *crucial*. They expressed themselves on the evaluation in words as follows:

... Language both reflects and forms our attitudes, and since the wholeness of the Church must include women in equal relationships, language will be either a barrier or an incentive for unity.

... It shapes the vision itself!

... Language is the question of what is real; language is the power of gods; it is essential and even critical!

There was not common agreement among all participants about the ways to resolve the difficult theological and liturgical issues with regard to language. The variety of perspectives represented indicated that for some the consultation pushed many into new explorations, while for others it was still not radical enough in confronting the "edge" of theological development. (What is progressive in some arenas is still too traditional in other contexts!) But it was indisputable to the participants that the language issue is not merely the province of culture or of Christian feminists, but has been claimed by leading and creative theologians (both male and female) who believe that "God-talk," the essence of their discipline, both reflects and shapes our faith, and that "inclusiveness" is crucial to the images and words we use to reflect on our faith. Surely those who have claimed that COCU's agenda is abstract, esoteric, and idealistic would have been convinced through their presence there that this issue is fundamental to church unity.

That the Consultation on Church Union provided the first arena for this encounter to take place *across denominations* and that it was centered totally in the issue of the *unity* of the Church as the Church speaks its own faith through liturgy marked a major advance for our churches as a whole. It will undoubtedly influence each of the communions as well, since many participants are playing key roles in the shaping of their own communions' work in the area.

Because the consultation was geared toward those who are policy and thought makers in their communions, a number of the participants were receiving their first exposure to the Consultation on Church Union. A major secondary value of the consultation was, "This experience has embodied COCU and the ecumenical reality for me. I want to find ways of being more a part of this enterprise." This was echoed in other ways; "There was a higher degree of excellence in this conference than I had anticipated; perhaps that is because it was COCU sponsored."

Those who participated in this consultation were left with many creative directions with which to proceed on the issues of exclusive — or inclusive — language in worship and theology. It is hoped that those who did not share in this event will be *equally* diligent in their attention to the Consultation's "alert" on sexism as one of the major barriers in our efforts toward church union.

Jeanne Audrey Powers

* * * * * * *

This collection of papers on the general theme of the relation between language and the worship of the church, and focusing especially on the problem of sexist church language about the people of God and about God, is the fruit of the Consultation on Language and Liturgy held in Nashville, Tennessee, more than a year ago. The Executive Committee of the Consultation on Church Union sponsored this gathering; it was organized and orchestrated by an ad hoc committee representing the Worship Commission, the Theology Commission, and the Women's Task Force of COCU.

It might be thought that papers presented in 1981 at a Consultation would have a half-life of about three days. This is not the case with the present collection. The Language and Liturgy Consultation was able to enlist the talents as major speakers and workshop leaders of a galaxy of leading experts in theology, linguistics, religious dance, Bible, hymnody, preaching — to name just a few. These are busy folk; the workshops, in particular, were presented without formal prepared papers. The very existence of this collection is therefore remarkable. More remarkable still is the continued timeliness of the content of the papers, and their amazing variety.

Participants in the consultation in Nashville will be reminded by the articles by Lewis Mudge, Gail Ramshaw Schmidt, and Sarah Bentley of things they heard — or perhaps, surfeited with so much richness of discourse in so little space, only half-heard. Since each participant could choose only two workshops to attend, those who elected Hymnody, for instance, were perhaps unable to take in the sessions on Strategies for Change in the Local Congregation. The papers and the ideas in them will therefore be new even to those who attended the Nashville meeting. They are as fresh today as they were when they were presented.

And, alas, the understanding among most church members on questions of sexism in the liturgy seems no higher today than last year. Several of the papers call attention to the fact that secular publishers and publications have adopted policies designed to remove sexist terms from schoolbooks and articles. The Church lags behind.

Perhaps these papers will be the basis of study groups on sexist language in congregations of the ten COCU denominations. On this particular question, the leaders seem to have left the rest of the parade far behind. The COCU consultation was hailed as the first ecumenical undertaking of its kind. This little booklet may be the vehicle for widespread ecumenical study of the words we use in speaking of and to God and God's people.

The editing of this collection is the work of Dr. William Watley, associate general secretary of COCU. His painstaking, sometimes frustrating, job was complicated or simplified as you will, by the fact that he was not present at the original consultation in Nashville. Dr. Gerald Moede, who was there, and I, who was there also, have put in our suggestions and caveats. My understanding of the whole issue of sexist language was expanded at Nashville. Reading these papers, and marvelling at their wide range, and pioneering depth, I have found my horizons expanding again.

Janet Harbison Penfield

Chair, Consultation on Language and
Liturgy and Women's Task Force

Major Addresses

A Call to Wholeness

Yvonne V. Delk

As a child I played a game in which I chanted over and over a call and a response.
The Call: What's the word?
The Response: Thunderbird.
The Call: What's the Price?
The Response: Forty-twice.

I didn't try to figure out the significance of the words. It was simply a chant that was easy to jump rope by. However, as I grew from childhood into adulthood, the opening line of the chant remained with me. What's the word, and more importantly, what's in a word? What power, value, and meaning do words convey?

I have come to realize that the words I use shape the way I see myself, see others, and the world of which I am a part. When I used the word "colored" to describe myself, it had no meaning for me. When I used the word "black" to describe myself, I had moved to a new level of understanding about myself; and even more important, I had discovered a word that conveyed a positive image about who I was. Now that I use the words African-American to describe my identity, I feel I have found words to convey the totality of who I am. The words are inclusive of my past, my present, and they express my hope for my future.

Words possess the power to call new worlds into being. Once we have heard them, we can longer remain the same. They open up new possibilities. They give new names and a new sense of mission and purpose in life.

In Isaiah 43:1, another construct is presented for understanding words and the power they hold. It is the construct of revelation, creation, and redemption. *Revelation comes first — but now says God, I am the one who created you*; revelation is followed by creation — *it is I who have formed you*; creation is followed by redemption — *fear not, for I have redeemed you; I have called you by name.*

Revelation, creation, and redemption, therefore, become words or constructs that provide glimpses into who we are, who God is, what we affirm about ourselves, our neighbor and our world, what we see and how we see it, what we are willing to do. The meaning of revelation, creation, and redemption is illustrated by the sermon-poem by James Weldon Johnson, "Creation."

In the poem, a liberating God is revealed; a God who calls into specificity that which is in obscurity. This is a God who brings into community that which is separated and isolated. James Weldon Johnson describes in vivid detail a God who yearns to be in relationship; who, in the midst of the void, decided to create, to call forth form and to speak the word that can become flesh and dwell upon the earth.

We can feel the power and passion of this God, being emptied into creation. Johnson describes a God who can smile and the light breaks; a God whose footsteps hollow the valleys and bulge the mountains. This is a God whose eyes blink and the lightning flashes, whose hands clap and the thunder rolls. This God speaks the words, "Bring forth," and fish and fowl, beasts and birds swim the rivers and the seas, roam the forests and the woods, and split the air with their wings.

1

However, after creating the earth and the heavens, the birds and the trees, rivers, sun, moon, and the stars, God is still lonely, still yearning for community, and decides to create that which can possess the image and likeness of God in human form.

James Weldon Johnson then describes this God kneeling into the dust and clay of the earth, like a mother who is bending over her baby; this is a God who is toiling and struggling to bring humankind into existence. But after all of God's work, the image lies dormant in the dust and clay. It cannot free itself from the dust and clay of which it is a part. The image is fixed, it is static, it is like a statue that has been cast into bronze. The image is frozen, locked in. It is closed. The image is domesticated, confined to a space, bound and trapped.

And God, looking at this image is still lonely, still yearning for community. And so this God, once again, knowing that this creation is not complete, kneels into the dust and breathes the breath of life, the wind of life, and the spirit of life into creation. At the moment this creation feels the breath, the wind, and the spirit of God, it begins to live. It has been freed from its trappings. It is now whole. It is free to love, to think, to feel, to act. It is freed from the powers that would seek to domesticate, control or contain it.

As I reflected on the meaning of revelation, creation, and redemption from the context of James Weldon Johnson's "Creation," I realized:

> The *revelation* of God for me was *of* one who frees us from all those forces which would seek to domesticate, contain, or control us.

> The *creation* for me was the feeling of the wind, breath, and spirit of God upon my countenance. It was a call to wholeness — calling out of obscurity into existence — giving me specificity and authorization to be, to exist.

> The *redemption* for me was the feeling of being set free to be the new creation who can, in turn, help to call into existence out of the void that which is something — that which can move and have its being.

The Question which faces us at this Language and Liturgy Conference is, "What's in a word?"

We have gathered to explore the meaning of Language and Liturgy, because we believe that it is in language, just as it is in God, that we live and move and have our being.

It is in language and liturgy that we experience revelation, creation, and redemption.

We are here because the language and liturgy in most of our churches is like the image of James Weldon Johnson's poem. It is trapped and domesticated by tradition, practices, culture, white, western, anglo-saxon, male views of the scripture and the world.

We are here to issue a call to wholeness. That call involves, first of all, *revelation: The revelation that we are not whole.* Our language and liturgy are trapped. They are domesticated. They are exclusive. They are limiting.

To define God as male is to limit God. It is obvious that women can no longer depend on a theology defined by men who are biased and prejudiced when it comes to women's rights.

The approach and treatment of male theologians have been shaped by the dominant climate of a male-dominated social culture. There is a need for a theology to emancipate the gospel from its maleness so that women can know the truth of the gospel as it applies to them.

A call to wholeness can mean no less than a return to the original languages of Hebrew, Greek, and Aramaic to recapture the feminine terms which have been overlooked or have not been translated accurately. A call to wholeness also involves a revelation that just as our language and liturgy is trapped by male imagery and perspectives, it is equally trapped by white western imagery and perspectives.

To define God as white is equally limiting to God.

It is obvious that people of color cannot depend on a theology defined by whites who are biased and prejudiced when it comes to the rights of people of color to be self-determining in a world-wide context. Many of our white churches have identified with the white majority who, in relation to people of color, have functioned as oppressors. White theology and white ecclesiology are creatures and products of American culture and, therefore, a culture-bound Christianity. They mirror the face of historic and universal racism as well as sexism.

A call to wholeness can mean no less than the willingness and the commitment to see the world and the gospel through eyes other than our own. A call to wholeness means, ultimately, that we cannot settle in language or liturgy for a world that is dominated by whites, by males, by the affluent, or by any one nationality.

To accept language or liturgy that is dominated, contained, or domesticated by gender or by race or by class as inclusive is to lose our grounding in community. It is to lose the sense of collective responsibility for that which is female as well as male, for that which is Black, Hispanic, Asian, Native American, as well as White. What takes its place is a vacuum in which community or relationships no longer exist. We become trapped forever in private destinies — doomed to whatever befalls us. In that void, wholeness vanishes completely. (Male replaces female, white replaces black.) What we lose is a part of ourselves, our understandings — our view of who we are and the purpose for which we were created. We lose each other. We lose the insights, understandings, perspectives of the other.

The world becomes diminished. The experience of God as female, as Black, as Hispanic, as Asian, as Native American, disappears and with it a part of existence, we return to the void, the nothingness that exists in the obscurity.

The call to wholeness, however, is more than revelation; it is a call to participate, to create.

Once we recognize that we are not whole, that a part of our existence is missing, that a part of our reality is trapped, contained, isolated, or domesticated, we move to the next step — that of creation. We join with God in the act of calling by name that which is missing into existence.

The 60's was a time of giving birth. Black Theology, Red Theology, Asian Theology, Hispanic Theology came into existence. Our language was changed and our liturgies changed as we received new names, new perspectives. We would not go back to the old order.

The 70's was a time of giving birth as women experimented with the power of naming — as we gave birth to words that allowed us choices:

From mother or mothers to parents;
From man to human beings; persons; everyone; or my word, folk;
From sons of God to children of God;
From kingdom to reign of God.

This conference becomes one more step in giving birth to language and liturgies that are inclusive, language that is whole.

Once the wind, spirit, and breath of God have been felt upon our countenance, we are no longer the same. Once a word has been spoken to us, over us, which calls us from being nobodies to being somebodies, we can no longer *be* the same. Once we have found our words, our names, *Nobody* — no institutions, no cultural practice, no tradition can reduce us to namelessness again. Language and liturgies give us an identity. They give us a mission and purpose in the world.

If we are females we can no longer ignore the existence of women as part of the people of God. We are no longer willing to be invisible partners, either in the work and life of the church and society, or in the interpretation and proclamation of the gospel.

The liberating word calls us into existence — into creation — and we can do no other than claim our existence in our language and our liturgies in the world.

The call to wholeness is not only revelation and creation, it is also redemption.

"Fear not, for I have redeemed you and when you pass through the waters, I will be with you. When you walk through the fire, you will not be consumed."

As we move to claim our names, to give birth to our language, to our perspectives, we face many risks.

The risk that we will be trivialized by the *status quo*;

The risk of being divided by race and class;

The risk of being limited by our own perspectives and insights. Our quest must lead us outward, not inward.

The redemptive word is the power of the gospel to renew our lives continually, opening us to freedom and to a future. Once the world has been revealed and once we have been called into existence, we move with the assurance that God is calling us into wholeness and we cannot go back to namelessness again. Roberta Flack, in an album, "I Told Jesus" says:

"I told Jesus that it would be alright if he changed my name."

Jesus said, "Child, the world won't know you if I change your name."

Roberta responds, "But I told Jesus that it would still be alright if he changed my name."

The redemptive word frees us to:

--Work for a more inclusive language, liturgy, church, and world.

—Take a prophetic stance over/against culture, tradition, history, practice.

—Understand and read the signs of the time as we participate in God's actions of justice and love.

What's the word that greets us as we come to this place at this hour? It is the call to wholeness today:

—From estrangement to reconciliation;

—From nothingness to somethingness;

—From obscurity to specificity.

The word is the call from our *past*:

—The call that led Mary in the Magnificat, to claim her name as blessed.

—The call that gave Esther the courage to confront the king.

—The call that empowered Sarah to give birth in her senior years.

—The call that freed Martha from the kitchen.

—The call that empowered Prudence Crandall to open a school in 1833 for young black women.

—The call that led Antoinette Brown Blackwell to present herself for ordination in 1853, becoming the first ordained woman minister of a recognized denomination in the United States.

—The call that gave Isabella Baumfree the courage to publicly challenge the evils of slavery, resulting in her name being changed to Sojourner Truth.

—The call that empowered daughters at all times and in all places to prophesy.

It is the call leading us to a new future:

—To become the word in flesh;

—To overcome our sexist, racist, classist angles, visions, and customs;

—To open ourselves to the breath, wind, and spirit of God which frees us from persons, institutions, systems, practices, cultural traditions that would domesticate or control or contain us.

In all times, the word is the call into existence of:

—Old and new names

—Old and new identities

—Old and new perspectives

—Old and new directions for the living of these days.

Let us pray:

Spirit of the Living God, fall afresh on us.

Spirit of the Living God, fall afresh on us.

Mold us, make us, free us, fill us, use us.

Spirit of the Living God, fall afresh on us.

Inclusive Language: Some Theological Reflections

Lewis S. Mudge

The organizing committee has given me a difficult task: that of combining the tone appropriate to "keynoting" with the style appropriate to contributing something of substance to the thinking of an already well-read and sophisticated audience. I take on this task only in the knowledge that we're in it together. Neither you nor I analyze the question of language in church life and liturgy from an Olympian distance. We do it as persons who at the very moment of the analysis, in the very process of reflection, are the Church of Jesus Christ.

My son Bill, now a college student, taught me that when he was four or five years old. He was always what we parents euphemistically call "an imaginative child." One evening, with no apparent provocation, he toddled into the living room and asked his mother and me, "Where are the rabbits?" Now, we had no actual rabbits among the family pets, so that was instantly identifiable as an "imaginative" question. "We don't know," we said gamely, "Where *are* the rabbits?" "Let's look," said young Bill. And so we began the search: first under chairs and tables, then behind draperies and in cabinets, and finally in bureau drawers. Up and down and around the apartment. "Where are the rabbits?" Finally, reassembled in the living room, and after a wise silence, our young Bill announced, "We're the rabbits!"

Just so. We who look for answers to theological questions are already the ones in whom, by grace, the answers are to be worked out. The object of our investigations may be "out there," but it is also "in here," in this room. That, after all, is part of what is meant by "living our way to unity." But because the object of our inquiry is in part ourselves and in our relationships, the possibility of distortion in the search is real. As is true for the physicist using the insights of quantum mechanics, investigation of a reality system also disturbs that system, introducing the biases and perspectives of the investigator into the object of inquiry. Somewhere there is a limit to our ability to see an object which is simultaneously ourselves as clearly as we would like. There is no escape from this problem. There is only the chance of limiting its influence by being aware of it.

I

The mandate of this consultation has gone through several redactions, but the point is clear enough. The over-all concern is to "weave the concerns of the Sexism Alert into the main fabric of the work of COCU as we move into a new and critical stage of living our way towards union." The language of the Alert reminds us that "the most subtle and significant threat sexism poses for the future of COCU is the possibility of a loss of new life . . . (Some) creative Christians can no longer give any legitimacy to the polarizing sexism that permeates the language and practice of worship, theology, styles of ministry, and the governing structures of all denominations." Within this range of issues, our assigned task is to focus on the issue of language: for, in the words of the Alert, "We believe that language is a key to understanding and shaping people's perception of themselves. Language is formative."

There can be no question of the need for this consultation. One wonders, indeed, if there is not a place for consultations of similar nature dealing with the other Alerts as well. Such will take place if there are those with the energy, determination, and organizing ability displayed already by the friends who have set up the present meeting. As chair of the Theology Commission I can testify that we fully "own" the Alerts, we regard their presence in the Consensus document as indispensable to that document's integrity, and yet also admit that in our day-to-day dialogue in drafting and defending the Consensus the Alerts seldom come specifically to the fore. In editing the main text of the Consensus we have gained in sensitivity to the question of inclusiveness: not only with respect to women and men, but also with respect to the handicapped and other minorities. The Consensus is unequivocal on the question of ordination of both women and men to every church office including that of bishop. And I believe that the document is free of sexist language. One has only to read ecumenical documents of as little as ten years ago, as well as many church documents even today, to realize how far we have come.

But no one would claim that we have fully incorporated the implications of this revolution into our thinking about the fundamental nature of the Church. There is, in short, much more here than simply ordaining women and cleaning up our language. The question of inclusive language is the vehicle for opening up questions concerning the meaning of the Church as social reality that we have never been asked by theologians, or anyone else for that matter, before the present decade. It is at this level that I want to engage us all for the next few minutes. In fact, I believe I will serve this consultation best if I do not reiterate all that has been said by feminist theologians and others, but try to place this movement, which we wholly share, in the modern history of Christian thought.

What has been the significance of this movement for inclusive language? It has clearly been the vehicle of an ethical concern, a concern for justice and the conviction that in the midst of society the church should exemplify that justice. The movement has also been part of the church's response to and participation in an important movement in our culture: a movement in which the contributions of both women and men have been seen as needed for fulness of corporate and symbolic life. But, most of all, I believe the movement for inclusive language has been the vehicle of a fundamental revolution in theological method which will have an impact on everything we do. The use of inclusive language forces us to think new thoughts about what it means to say that Jesus Christ has transformingly entered our history, the fabric of our sociality. The primary objective of this paper is to make clear what that means.

II

What *does* it mean? To assist us on the way to an answer, let me suggest a frame of reference consisting of three propositions: (a) that the question central to the theological problematic of the 19th and 20th centuries is the question of the humanity of God; (b) that the most fruitful approach to this question today is through what might be called ecclesio-sociology; (c) that a fundamental point of access to what is going on as *ekklesia* forms in society lies in the analysis of the church's language. Let us take each proposition in turn.

(a) *The question of the humanity of God.* I say that the central problem is that of the "how" of God-with-us. There is no space within this essay to review Western theology's long struggle with the problem of God in relation to historical relativity. From the enlightenment on, and especially since what is coming to be called the "second enlightenment" or rise of critical-historical method, we have struggled with the question of how finite forms of expression in any medium — linguistic, social, institutional — can be vehicles of the divine. For all such expressions are subject to change over time and space. All vary in relationship to other factors in the human realm. None exhibits traits, or in principle can do so, which mark it as manifestation of the divine. This problem has nowhere been more acute than in the area of biblical scholarship. Without going into well-known detail, we can say that God enters into and acts in the midst of the history of the human. How can such an assertion make sense in terms of the life we know?

(b) *The contribution of "ecclesio-sociology."* It is less widely agreed, but basic to my own position, that this question of the humanity of God is helpfully approached today through the question of ecclesiology in society. Now this assertion could easily be misunderstood. I do not mean to take us down the garden path to any form of ecclesiastical absolutism, or to any notion of the church's otherworldly character and still less of an idea of the infallibility of its teaching office. No, I am rather saying that we must work out the question of the humanity of God ecclesiologically because the church's social form is fundamental to its faith and witness. The assumptions of our community and culture about what a "church" is no longer give us answers in these matters we can take for granted.

I have in mind, of course, Ernst Troeltsch's characterization of the whole post-Enlightenment period in the famous final chapter of his *Social Teachings of the Christian Churches and Groups*. Troeltsch's main concern for almost a thousand pages has been the ecclesio-ethical interactions of the gospel with society. He argues that the two great patterns of interaction — that of the Middle Ages and that of the synthesis we know today as the "protestant ethic," together with the various forms of sectarian protest against them — are no longer meaningful in a society which since 1800 or so has become increasingly individualistic and increasingly pluralistic. Nevertheless, ecclesiastical forms associated with the defunct interactions between gospel and society — basically the "catholic" and "protestant" forms with which we are familiar — remain in existence because we have nothing better. We are in this respect "parasitic" upon the past. If we are to find a form of interaction appropriate to modernity, Troeltsch argues, "thoughts will have to be thought which have not yet been thought."

Troeltsch's basic insight, of course, is that what the gospel generates in history is not merely a set of beliefs or doctrines but an ecclesio-ethical reality which takes some sort of concrete form in relation to social structures and the cultural achievements that occur within and legitimate them. It is plain that this had begun to be understood a century earlier by Schleirmacher in one way and by Hegel in another. This history of the determination to think out the humanity-of-God problem ecclesially can be traced, then, through Albrecht Ritschl, Karl Barth, Dietrich Bonhoeffer, H. Richard Niebuhr, and most recently, Edward Farley, who teaches at Vanderbilt Divinity School.

8

I have come to the point of saying that the covenantal community of faith is itself the primary form in which the gift of grace comes. Grace is the possibility of living in a community which anticipates the final gathering of humanity under the rule of God. Grace comes to us through a particular network of relationships. It is "the gift of membership." It comes in and through the way we are mutually constituted as human beings in the midst of a world of "graceless" powers: We are called, as Dietrich Bonhoeffer put it, to be "Jesus Christ existing in the form of a community." The question of the possibility of the existence of such a community — of the existence of a community "in Christ" whose characteristics permit us to speak in a sense-making way of its being the locus of the humanity of God in the midst of the humanity of this world — is not a speculative question but an ecclesio-ethical question.

(c) *That the best approach to critical study of this ecclesio-ethical reality is through the way it generates and uses language.* The elaboration of this point will occupy us in the next section of this paper. Meanwhile let me acknowledge that there is much in human relationships besides language. We make a methodological error if we focus attention on language alone. For one thing, we may overlook the whole problem of "false consciousness." Simply expressed this means that what we say may be a covert justification for the power position we represent. Yet there are both empirical and theoretical advantages in taking language as our starting point. Empirically, language is the vehicle through which the structures and symbol systems of a society are set in operation in the day-to-day interactions by which the social reality in question is sustained. And, of course, it is important that the primary evidence we have for the life of the early church is linguistic. If our Bible study and study of the life of the church in society can follow parallel methods, we will be ahead. And then, too, attention to the language of the church has political momentum today, which offers the hope that academic efforts in this field could make a contribution.

III

We have now established our basic terms of reference. To summarize: language is a key to the church's reality in society, and that reality is where we look for the signs of the "humanity of God." Our task is to understand how God brings a redeemed historical-social humanity into being, and to grasp the significance of the question of inclusive language in this context.

It will be easier to say what we mean by a "redeemed" humanity if we know what we mean by "humanity" in the first place. This, today, is a more difficult question than it may at first appear to be. It is notorious, of course, that when Christian theologians of past generations spoke of "man" they had in mind mostly male human beings of their own class and culture. Even philosophical conceptions of the human may sometimes be traced back to such specific, uncriticized, assumptions. But we are not in a much better position with today's human sciences, which are not only for the most part Western, and thus have built-in cultural bias, but exhibit various forms of cognitive interest, and therefore cognitive bias, as well. What is more, the human sciences carve humanity up without putting us back together again. Sociology, psychology, anthropology and the rest are seemingly grounded in mutually incompatible epistemologies. The question of the nature of the human waits for a solution to the question of the unity of the human. And this is where language, as a potentially universal medium of human communication, may open the door.

If we wish, then, to say what we mean by "humanity" in connection with "the humanity of God" we must transcend not only the traditional theological anthropologies, but also what the human sciences provide. I suggest that we begin with an empirical observation so simple that it may at first disappoint you: humanity is all these people, men and women, four or five billion of them, whom we can locate and count and whom we must feed. While we may be in difficulty at the point of giving a theoretical definition of the human, humanity as such has for the first time become subject to empirical observation. We have the capacity now to name and number the human race with computers. Just as it makes a difference to our imaginations to see the earth from space, so it makes a difference to realize that "humanity" could, if we wished, be a list of names!

Second, let us realize that "humanity" does not have a common essence, unless we somehow collectively choose one. Humanity is becoming what it will be. The decisions and actions of all these human beings will determine what humanity will be. The question of what humanity will be is therefore open to the dimensions of freedom, and of grace.

And, third, we must come to understand that we will be what we will be because of the way we constitute each other as persons through our words and actions, and that these words and actions represent our understanding of the power situation in which we stand.

Our actions in relation to each other grow out of perceptions of our own power as well as out of our perceptions of the power or powers we have ranged over against us. Our perception of our own power arises not only from a fundamental inner sense of ourselves but also from our experience up to that point in human interaction. We never come on the human scene *de novo*. We always find a set of power relationships already existing, which are the result of the patterns of interaction of past generations. And we never leave the human scene unaffected. Our interpretation of the power possibilities we find for our lives leads to patterns of activity which in turn affect the power-sense of generations to come.

The role of language in this humanity-forming process is obvious. Language is the most sophisticated layer of the symbolic medium in which we human beings exist. It is the layer most subject to our manipulation and hence most subject to conscious opening to possibilities not yet realized, to utterances at variance with present social reality. The importance of this last point will emerge later. But if language is the most sophisticated and supple layer of our symbolic medium, it is not the only layer. In fact, language is the medium in which other sorts of signs become consciously structured and utilized. We live in an ocean of pre-linguistic signs, some of the most potent of which are the cultural and social monuments we produce as a result of the decisions we make in our human interactions.

Let us illustrate. Suppose that we discover that we have the capability of extracting oil from the ground and that by organizing others for the purpose of obtaining this substance, refining it, and marketing it we have produced a complex

10

pattern of repeated interaction we call a corporation. A pattern of activity of this sort contains within itself a complex network of ways in which persons construe others as persons and are construed in return. These forms of construal, attached as they are to profit-making activities are also patterns of power. These patterns proliferate and radiate outward as other persons found similar or interacting activities. Soon human habitations called cities with structures like Chicago's Standard Oil Building spring up. We eventually have a series of cultural monuments which are signs of the existence in the human sphere of certain ways of conceiving power and persons. The "humanity" that grows up in such a context will live within a communication network that transmits messages of a certain kind. If the language-in-use of a society so organized is analyzed, it should reveal something of the way sense-making action within that society is construed by its citizens.

But language here is only the sophisticated, self-conscious surface of the system of signs that lies underneath. Paul Ricoeur has indeed argued that we can not only analyze the language found in a society's work "texts but we can also investigate the underlying patterns of behavior and the monuments — like the Standard Oil Building — which that behavior has produced. We can see these patterns as 'text-like'." What the human sciences are really doing, says Ricoeur, is "reading" the messages transmitted by the "signs" which a given society produces in the process of doing what it does. Thus we may penetrate to the depth dimension of language. What finds its way into actual language is conscious communication existing in a still larger nexus of unconscious communication which we can nevertheless "read" and be made conscious of if we have the sensitivity to do so.

Now it is clear that in any society, in any such nexus of conscious and unconscious signs, some persons and some sorts of human experience, will have greater access to the social communications medium than others. Jurgen Habermas, the German social theorist, has dramatized the way in which this is so by use of a heuristic concept he calls the "ideal speech situation." This, in a word, is the notion of a social reality in which all participants, and all tracts and forms of human experience, have equal access to the social sign-system both in its pre-linguistic and linguistic forms. It is a situation, we would say, in which all find the social system able to articulate that which is most important to them, what is most basic to their lives, as well as the experiences which they have every day.

Analysis of the language in use in both church and society in the West today shows numerous systematic departures from Habermas' "idea speech situation." On the contrary, what we have are examples, at every turn, of what he calls "systematically distorted communication." In "systematically distorted communication" we no longer have a "symmetrical distribution of chances to choose and to apply speech-acts." No longer do "all potential participants in a discourse have the same chance to initiate and sustain dialogue through questions and answers, claims and counterclaims." In the face of this distortion, certain preconceptions, certain kinds of experience of life, remain excluded from consideration.

Translating Haberman's conceptuality into our own, we may say that under these circumstances the power structures of the society and the imaginative forms that go with them are such that the system of communication places certain potential members of the dialogue at a disadvantage. The language system that has grown out of this pattern of social imagination, and which serves to sustain it in being inter-subjectively, contains a series of usages which shut certain perspectives, certain human experiences, out of the communication system. What we call "sexist language" is language framed in such an exclusionary usage. But sexist language is not the only form of "systematically distorted communication." In the "language" of the present international monetary system, to choose one example among many, there is an exclusionist tendency toward messages which do not conform to the precon-ceptions of the bankers and the multinational corporations. And so on, and so on.

Perhaps this is enough to suggest that the analysis of sexist language is merely the furthest advanced of the language analyses available at the present time.

We should also consider racist language, the language of congregational exclusivism, and the language of institutionalism, to name the other COCU "Alerts." Each could usefully be analyzed in the same terms. In each case we would see that what we call "humanity" and the redemption of humanity through the gathering of a People of God are at stake in these matters of language which at first seemed so simple.

IV

Let us take stock. I am reminded of the experience of finding myself lying on the X-ray table in the local hospital, readied for a particularly odious diagnostic examination, when the specialist came in rubbing his hands genially and saying, "Now, Mr. Mudge, why are we doing all this?" My reply was something to the effect of saying, "If you don't know, I'm getting out of here." Well, why all this analysis after the manner of Habermas and Ricoeur? Only to return to our original intention, which was to illuminate the ecclesial expression of "the humanity of God" through analysis of the world's and the church's language.

It is tempting, indeed, to relate the Church more or less directly to Habermas' notion of the "ideal speech situation," the condition of systematically undistorted communication. After all, Habermas himself tells us that this means an overcoming of repression, the discovery of the socio-linguistic correlates for truth, freedom, and justice. But let us not forget that the "ideal speech situation" is for Habermas a heuristic device for analyzing the anything-but-ideal speech-reality in which we live. It is not clear that he regards it as an actual, attainable, state. For us to turn a heuristic device into a correlate for the Kingdom of God would smack of a kind of docetism. We will not get rid of the reality of power, and where there is power and interest we will have distortion in the speech situation. For communication in the ideal speech situation to be anything but trivial, we must wrestle with these questions of power, not ignore them.

Let's take a hypothetical problem which may make this clear. We have said that "humanity is literally all these people." Today, for the first time, we begin to be able to have an empirical notion of humanity, rather than the notion of humanity as abstract essence which appears in our creeds, because we can state the conditions under which the whole of humanity might literally be tuned into a single communications network. Such might be possible through simultaneous translation and the transistor radio. Now suppose we had such a hookup and were faced with the question of what we would say. The first problem, of course, would be that if the hookup were *ours* and *we* were doing the saying there would be a systematic distortion of communication from the start. Only if the hookup belonged to all, and if everyone had the capacity for both initiating communication and answering back would we have the possibility of undistorted communication.

All right, let's suppose we had that possibility too. Now what should we talk about? What should we talk about in order to have everybody in the dialogue? The danger, it becomes clear, is that the more profound the topic is for some the more incomprehensible it is to others. Here is an interesting experiment to try in class. What would *you* say to start the dialogue? One of my students suggested a profound question. She said we should transmit over the human communications network the traditional Chinese greeting: "Have you eaten?" To which the traditionally polite, but always truthful, Chinese answer is "Yes I have." But would most North Americans understand? Or understand soon enough? Suppose we were to say, "What hath God wrought?" How would the Chinese hear that? The danger, you see, is that to count on universal understanding we might have to resort to "How do you hear me? Loud and clear? Five by five! Roger. How's the weather there? Good here, too!"

The problem is that the ideal speech situation tends to allow only trivial communication. Why? Because symbolic content of real human importance, symbolic content which invokes the dimensions of depth in human experience, which raises questions such as the character of our basic trust in the goodness of life, is invariably deeply embedded in cultures and literatures themselves shaped over centuries by the power questions in relation to which they have grown up. How may we build "humanity" into our theology in such a way that "everyone is in," and yet not make this "humanity" trivial in content? How to realize the humanity of God where the humanity in question is represented symbolically in terms of the depths of human experience? How to express this inclusive understanding of humanity, indeed, when we realize that the depth questions arise precisely from the struggle with the meaning of power: my own capacity and its sources, power over against me, power expressed in the structure of church and state, the ultimate power with which I have to do?

V

I want, in closing, to sketch the beginning of an answer to this difficult question. The old and new covenants, the covenants of Moses and the covenant of Jesus Christ, have the impact of removing certain profound aspects of human experience, certain human symbols, from contexts of power which are essentially tribal or parochial to a power context which is ultimate or universal because it is that of the God above all tribal Gods. This removal effects a transformation of the imaginative form in which the power issue is articulated. Let us take some examples. The impact of the covenant-making described in the book of Exodus was, among many other things, to transfer the meaning of murder from the context of tribal blood-revenge to the context of the universal power of Yahweh expressed in and through a tribal federation in which the rights of "otherness," i.e., human reality outside one's own tribe, are guaranteed and in which the power of Yahweh is at first identified with no single human power center. The question of murder departs from the tribal power-context and enters the trans-tribal and eventually universally human context.

Or, think of the New Covenant. The significance of the death and resurrection of Christ is to make all that Jesus stood for, the whole array of depth responses he evoked together with the array of culturally transmitted symbols connected with these responses, become extraterritorial to both the Jewish and Roman power centers of the time. This, of course, is done at great cost. The messianic banquet in the Kingdom of God is represented on earth at the Last Supper, which leads to resurrection only through crucifixion. Both the extraterritoriality of the Old Covenant and that of the New involve sacrifice for the sake of a new humanity coming to be.

Now we may begin to draw the threads of this argument together. Clearly, the creation of a universal human nexus is possible only if that which is most essential to humanity moves from the parochial power contexts of society, tribe, and nation to an incorporation into God's purposes which make it truly "the humanity of God." And that "humanity of God" is represented on earth, in turn, by a community, an *ekklesia*, which is precisely a space where the human depths becomes universally sharable across cultures by passage through crucifixion and resurrection. How is this last possible? Do we mean that given forms of the human imagination somehow become universal? No, for that would be imperialism. Rather, the forms of human imagination are deconstructed down to their sources and reconstructed — a kind of death and resurrection of culture — so that they are freed from parochial limitation and can henceforth function as parts of a systematically undistorted language system.

In adopting covenantal imagery for the new steps it will take toward unity, COCU has hold of something of immense potential power that, I am convinced, it has only begun to understand. For the basis of a truly profound version of the "ideal speech situation," a network of human communication truly undistorted by alienating power relationships, can only be built if that which is deepest in human experience is separated from our tribal national, gender-specific, forms of the will-to-power and connected with the will for all humankind of the God to whom alone is the glory. It is not enough to suppress the will-to-power. We must offer it up, and to do so we must learn again the human meanings of the rituals of sacrifice, on the altar, on the cross. As I recently heard a feminist theologian say, "Power means taking control of our lives so we can give them away."

Could we not, as the New Israel, once again begin to think what it might mean to offer ourselves as what Isaiah called "a new covenant of the peoples," a people like the Israel of old leading a movement of renunciation of the warring Canaanite city-states all about us, seeking to be instruments of a universal human covenant against war, against exploitation and oppression, against hunger, and against every language that makes these things seem natural and inevitable? Could we not make ourselves a world-wide movement of people to join hands in a covenant of peace? Let us not forget that covenant imagery is fundamental not only for us, but also in the sacred scriptures of Judaism and Islam. That would at least be a starting point. There is enough "otherness" for us there to curb our unwitting imperialisms, and enough possibility that we might well devote the rest of our lives under God to finding a truly inclusive human language.

De Divinis Nominibus: The Gender of God

Gail Ramshaw Schmidt

How does human language name God? Which revealed words has the tradition canonized, and how do the faithful verbally express and interpret their relationship with God? "You shall not make yourself a graven image," it was said. Yet more solid than stone, more resistant to iconoclasm than bronze, are the images cast in theological language and so engraved on our minds and throughout our prayers. We must always be inquiring whether the tendency of theological language toward immutability is wholly a healthy one. It is to that theological language which names God as "he" that this inquiry is addressed.

With the phrase *de divinis nominibus*, on the divine names, we recall both Dionysius and Thomas Aquinas.[1] It is with both that we must converse, the elaborate metaphors of Christian imagery and the reasoned discourses of systematic theologians. We know that Christian poets and mystics have a rare ability to talk to and of God in unique ways. But by definition their vision is a private one, and while we admire Dionysius' *via negativa* or Julian of Norwich's praise of Jesus as Mother, we do not employ their writings in public prayer. Offshoots of Christianity more intrigued by metaphor than by dogma enjoy a release from canonized language, but the Gnostics were anathematized, the Shakers have died out, and Jung was hardly a worshiping church member. Heinrich Ott's recent theological study of God as person notes correctly that problems in naming God arise in conversation *about* God. Hence he urges conversation *to* God.[2] Yet he writes about the safety of direct address in language which is unquotably sexist. We are responsible at least for the language we engrave on the minds and prayers of others. While like the Cistercians we realize the inadequacy of language, we must also like the Cistercians choose some language with which to pray faithfully.

Conversations about the naming of God as Father are becoming increasingly common,[3] and recently publications have pointed to the difficulty in calling God "he."[4] But serious investigation into the gender of God has not proceeded very far. About God's gender it is far easier to hold an impassioned opinion than to articulate a reasoned argument or a reasonable solution. This study will address the "God-he" problem with the following questions: How does language talk of God? How has the Judeo-Christian tradition named God's gender, and why? How does gender function in modern American English? What are the alternatives to calling God he? If we agree

---

[1] Thomas Aquinas, *Summa Theologiae 1a. 13,1.*

[2] Heinrich Ott, *God*, tr. Iain and Ute Nicol (Atlanta: John Knox 1974).

[3] For example: *God as Father?* e. Johannes-Baptist Metz and Edward Schillebeeckx, *Concilium* 143 (New York: Seabury 1981), and Krister Stendahl, "Enrichment or Threat? When the Eves Come Marching In," *Sexist Religion and Women in the Church: No More Silence!* ed. Alice Hageman (New York: Association 1974) 117-123.

[4] Letty Russell, "Changing Language and the Church," *the Liberating Word* (Philadelphia: Westminster 1976) 92-93; Marianne Sawicki, *Faith and Sexism: Guidelines for Religious Educators* (New York: Seabury 1979) 19-23.

Reprinted by permission from the March, 1982 issue of *Worship*.

that refusing to examine our engraved speech leads to an idolatry more sophisticated but no less culpable than that with the golden calf, we have at least begun at the same place.

"All I have written seems to me like so much straw compared with what I have seen and what has been revealed to me." With these words Thomas Aquinas admitted the inadequacy of words to describe God, and he ceased work on the Summa Theologiae. While some may suggest that we need no words to address God in the interior of our heart, human beings do require words at least to talk together to and of God. In searching for the best words to use, we turn first to Thomas' discussion of theological language. For despite his final disclaimer of language, and despite his sexism much derided by shocked moderns, he investigates the naming of God with a clarity which has undergirded all subsequent inquiry. For critical historical study has shown that a thinker can be entirely brilliant on one subject — say, linguistic philosophy — while being completely wrongheaded on another — say, women.

How does language talk of God? In the linguistic philosophy of the ancient Near East, a thing had no reality prior to its naming. This theory has been adapted in modern philosophy as the theory of the interrelationship between language and reality. That is, we know as we name. But God, Genesis claims, is prior to language. The divine is beyond the human, outside our categories. In some religions, the sacred is held so far beyond the secular that a wholly separate language is employed for worship and theology. But the self-revelation of our God in history and the incarnation of Christ Jesus encourages Christians to talk of God in their finest vernacular speech.

One recent study of God's gender suggests that modern Christianity can talk directly of God and so need not use anthropomorphisms in worship and theology.[5] Besides sounding naively optimistic about human maturity, this suggestion has not deeply understood language. Human language cannot express the essence of God, nor its power effect communication with God, any more than the human mind can grasp at divinity. Different languages and genres use various techniques to varying degrees in their worship and theology. Aquinas begins his discussion of theological language by describing metaphoric use of language, and we shall begin with him there.

"Holy Scripture delivers spiritual things to us beneath metaphors taken from bodily things."[6] We talk of divine truth as though human categories applied; thus we are talking of two quite different things — the human and the divine — simultaneously. Theological language is to great degree metaphoric talk: language which is open to associations, which encourages insight and facilitates disclosure by its linking of disparate things.[7] "God is said to have no name, or to be beyond naming, because his essence is beyond what we understand of him and the meaning of the names we use."[8] We speak the metaphors with utter humility, believing in the God beyond the words and concluding our metaphoric speech to be so much straw.

---

[5] Sheila D. Collins, *A Different Heaven and Earth* (Valley Forge, Penn.: Judson 1974) 217.

[6] Aquinas, *Summa* 1a. I, 9.

[7] Mark Searle, "Litury as Metaphor," *Worship* 55 (1981) 98-120; Gail Ramshaw Schmidt, "Liturgy as Poetry: Implications of a Definition," *Living Worship* 15 (October 1979) no. 8.

[8] Aquinas, *Summa* Ia. 13, I.

Metaphors can be anthropomorphic. That is, we can talk of God as though God were a woman or a man or a child or a people. We ascribe to God breasts or a strong arm or a shining countenance. We use personification when we ascribe to God personal characteristics: anger, delight, speech, age. Nonhuman metaphors are common in the Judeo-Christian tradition. Interestingly, we speak of God as an animal or a natural phenomenon more easily than as a woman: God has wings, God belches fire. The Psalms were bold in objectifying divinity. "Rock" recurs often in the Psalms as a metaphor for God.

Aquinas offers metaphoric language the test of contradictability. "It is part of the meaning of 'rock' that it has its being in a merely material way. Such words can be used of God only metaphorically."[9] God is a rock: but of course God is *not* a rock. Nor has God a shining countenance or milk-filled breasts. The power of metaphor can tease us into believing the reality of our human language, and the East has employed more than the West the *via negativa*, the God-is-not speech. But even if we say God is not light, the technique of objectification is present despite the disclaimer.

Literature professors teach the proper interpretation of metaphoric language. The reader must be honest to the metaphor and not press it beyond its intent. "We are the hollow men / We are the stuffed men / Leaning together / Headpiece filled with straw"[10] does not imply that we are literally scarecrows. Nor does metaphoric talk of God as mother mean that in any essential way God is half female or acts in some stereotypically feminine manner. We must be careful of anecdotes about God's sitting up in the sky on his throne or pictures of God as two men and an amorphous third. Metaphoric language must always be contradicted. God is like a father, but a father who wills his son to die. God is like a castle: but as my two-year-old retorted, "God is not a castle. God is God."

In some contexts, naming God "he" is metaphoric. Sustained metaphors which liken God to a king might use "he" in the same metaphoric fashion (although "sovereign" sounds more noble and as a nonsex-specified noun would not require a "he"). Our recognizing the metaphoric nature of God-he language would be facilitated if we used God-she in similar constructions. It is God as she who calls us into the ways of wisdom. But the possibilities of this metaphoric language are limited. Too easily most human occupations — shepherd, judge, teacher — are assigned male pronouns, and objectifications are often assigned male pronouns, as in "Refuge, he." If only images of motherhood are granted female pronouns, we remain impoverished.[11] But even when the metaphoric use of pronouns is employed most creatively, there is still the contradictability: God is not he, God is not she.

Yet we must be bolder in our use of metaphors for God. In the disclosure of surprising metaphors we meet God anew. The startling language invites us to conversion. Reviving biblical metaphors ought not to be as controversial or risky as it apparently is. To ascribe to God a full range of human activity and emotions; to

---

[9] Aquinas, *Summa* Ia. 13, 4.

[10] T.S. Eliot, "The Hollow Men," *The Complete Poems and Plays 1909-1950* (New York: Harcourt, Brace and World 1958) 60.

[11] Rita M. Gross, "Steps Toward Feminine Imagery of Deity in Jewish Theology," *Judaism* 30 (1981) 190-192.

balance in God the strength of God who reigns with the weakness of God who suffers; to objectify God; and finally to negate these images, pleading God-is-not: opening up God language will combat the incipient idolatry in one's traditional speech.

A second way that language talks of God is analogical. By analogy Aquinas means those verbal expressions by which we are trying to say what we mean. Of these statements one does not postulate the opposite. "Words like 'good' and 'wise' when used of God do signify something God really is, but they signify it imperfectly because creatures represent God imperfectly."[12] Our saying "God is good" is not countered by our saying "God is not good." Although our category "good" is inadequate to attach to God, we use such analogical language because through it we try to speak what we mean. Aquinas insists that in analogy the Christian revelation establishes the definition, and not the other way around. That is, we look to the Scriptures for a description of God as good, from which we arrive at our definition of good. This adaptation of Platonic idealism acts to correct our natural error of imagining a God in our own image and within our own language.

We are to be humble about language even in its most careful, creedal usage. God is called Father not, as a prominent fundamentalist preacher recently announced, because otherwise the American family structure will further erode. Rather, God is named Father because in the revealed tradition Jesus called God Abba, and to that extraordinary religious event we struggle to attach human words. In the inaccurate translation of Abba into Father we see that human words are a far cry from the divine reality revealed in the seminal stories of the faith.

Trinitarian language is analogous language. The naming of the three persons of the Trinity, the calling of relationships within God, uses language which tries to say God's self-naming. All relational language concerning God is analogous. When we say that God relates not only within God's self but also with humankind, we use analogous language. Some usages of God-he language are similarly analogous. The revelation says that the Judeo-Christian God is a relational being, a God known as who, not which. The tradition has tried to say this by rejecting the pronoun "it" and using instead "he," always in this analogous usage recognized as a nonsex-specific but personal pronoun. While we can appreciate the historic intent of this language, it remains to be seen whether it is any longer possible.

Only when analogy, as Wolfhart Pannenberg says, open up to mystery, only when our language of God leads to awed doxology, are we recognizing the limits of human language in its speech of God.[13] When in a homily an anecdote about a father-child relationship or about the birth process affirms a basic similarity with God, the simile has shrunk our God. Always in analogy what is unlike is more than what is like. Theological sensitivity in explicating analogical language frees us from distortions and helps point to the glory of God. If we would grant often in our speech that "he" is wholly inadequate as a personal pronoun in referring to God, much of our difficulty would be lessened. Instead, we hear vociferous defense of this masculine designation, as if it were in some way true.

---

[12] Aquinas, *Summa* Ia. 13, 2.
[13] Wolfhart Pannenberg, "Analogy and Doxology," *Basic Questions in Theology*, tr. George H. Kehm (Philadelphia: Fortress 1972) I, 215.

Edward Schillebeeckx talks of the kerygma breaking the human models.[14] He sees that human language has developed God talk, but that Christianity breaks apart that language even while being required to use it. With Jesus, he writes, we use the models of Messiah or of Wisdom; yet the models are admittedly inadequate, and even in some cases inappropriate, to the reality made known in Christ. So with all God talk: the models provided by human speech are recast by the proclamation of our God. It is not only, as Ian Ramsey notes, that paradox exists within the parts of the divine title, that "God" and "Father" are opposite to one another and stand in creative tension.[15] It is even, Schillebeeckx would say, that the meanings of the individual words are shattered, that "God" and "Father" are broken by the reality of the cross. It is time that we examine the model of God-he for its undoing by the cross.

Several recent studies provide thorough discussions of how God's gender was expressed throughout the Judeo-Christian tradition. Leonard Swidler offers a concise treatment of the relationship between the worship of Yahweh and of Asherah and then lists biblical, extrabiblical, rabbinic, and historic Christian references to the "feminine" aspect of God.[16] Other scholars have tried to account for the pattern of masculine language for God.[17] While this essay cannot be the place for a detailed historical study, we can review the most important aspects of the history of the naming of God's gender.

All the languages formative in the Judeo-Christian tradition had grammatical gender. That is, all nouns and pronouns were assigned, either naturally, logically, or arbitrarily, to grammatical categories called gender. Sometimes a noun's grammatical gender was elaborated upon for poetic purposes, and sometimes we can guess why a certain inanimate object was assigned its specific gender. But in languages with grammatical gender there is no actual significance in gender designation. That a table is feminine does not mean that the table has female sexuality or that it is necessarily related to a characteristically feminine realm. Hebrew, Aramaic, Greek, and Latin all have grammatical gender. In polytheistic cultures, the assigning of masculine gender to the word god is evident from the word goddess, which, as in poet-poetess, is a diminutive form. Perhaps the cultural pattern of male domination in religious matters was a, or the, significant cause. But it remains that the assignment of masculine grammatical gender does not prove anything about a supposed sexuality of the Judeo-Christian God. Hebrew and Christian theologians insisted that their God was not of one or both sexes but was beyond sexuality. Gregory of Nazianzus addresses specifically the question of masculine gender of God and ridicules those who would draw from the gender designation a notion of actual sexuality within God.[18] Aquinas,

[14] Edward Schillebeeckx, *Interim Report on the Books Jesus and Christ* (New York: Crossroad 1981) 24, passim.

[15] Ian Ramsey, *Religious Language* (New York: Macmillan 1963) 203-205.

[16] Leonard Swidler, *Biblical Affirmations of Women* (Philadelphia: Westminster 1979) 21-73.

[17] For example: Paul D. Hanson, "Masculine Metaphors for God and Sex-Discrimination in the Old Testament," *The Ecumenical Review* 27 (1975) 317-321, and Elaine H. Pagels, "What Became of God the Mother? Conflicting Images of God in Early Christianity," *Womanspirit Rising: A Feminist Reader in Religion*, ed. Carol P. Christ and Judity Plaskow (New York: Harper and Row 1979) 107-119.

[18] Gregory of Nazianzus, "The Fifth Theological Oration: On the Spirit," *Christology of the Later Fathers*, The Library of Christian Classics, Vol. 3, ed. E.R. Hardy and C.C. Richardson (Philadelphia: Westminster 1954) 198.

also, in defending the expression "He who is" as the most appropriate name for God, states that the term "does not signify any particular form, but rather existence itself."[19] Aquinas assumes here that the pronoun "he" does not suggest the form of the human male.

A second important aspect of the historic situation is that in the ancient world, the Judeo-Christian God stands counter to polytheism, in which there was a powerful supply of female gods. In both the Old and New Testaments, Yahweh God, the Father of Jesus Christ, opposes a significant cult of the female god, and the biblical proclamation includes polemic against the sexual rituals offered before the female god. We are now studying the effects of this situation on the proclamation. Furthermore, the written documents and the cultural patterns within which Judaism and Christianity developed indicate a deeply engrained sexism, and we are only beginning to estimate to what degree and in what ways this cultural sexism influenced theological thought and expression.

Recent studies are showing us the openness of this sexist tradition to feminine gender for God. There are the oft-cited biblical references to God as woman. Jewish tradition, in its reluctance to speak directly of God, relied increasingly in its speech on feminine personifications of God. Law is hypostatized as Torah, God's presence as *shekinah*, wisdom as *hokmah*, and spirit as *ruah*. We do not know, however, how much the female personifications of these words affected theology and proclamation. It is not clear how this tradition can be imported into modern English, in which these words are not in any respect "feminine." The pattern remained, even in this tradition, that a mascline god possessed feminine characteristics. Finally, while it is illuminating and potentially corrective to read about deviant traditions, like the Gnostics, the Jewish mystics, and the Shakers, in which radical measures were tried in the naming of God's gender, the idiosyncracies of those traditions make any appropriation of their attempts unrealistic.

Recent use of the word person in association with God has unfortunately tightened the tie between God and male sexuality. In the classic Christian formulations, the word person was a technical term which meant something like mode of being. God has three persons: that is, God has three ways of being within the one being of God. There are relationships within God. Language of Father and Son had to do with relations within the being of God, not with relationships between God and the faithful.

But in the last century theology has spoken of God as personal, and even of God as person. At the start this reflected relationships between God and humankind. But increasingly talk of God as person is influenced by modern definitions of person as a self-conscious being, and different theologians can stress quite different things when referring to God as person. Ott refers to God's mutuality with humankind.[20] Pannenberg defines God's personhood as God's nonmanipulability (a highly rationalistic definition of person, I might add).[21] But language of God as person can lead to images of God as a superperson, and then all too easily to God as a supermale.

---

[19] Aquinas, *Summa* Ia. 13, 11.

[20] Ott, *God* 42.

[21] Pannenberg, *Basic Questions,* I, 232.

Finally the word person is linked in modern American English to human personality, and we find ourselves open to anthropomorphism of the cheapest sort.

In recent debates concerning the ordination of women a dangerous example of this erroneous use of person surfaced. The priest's likeness to Christ spilled over into talk of the priest as a symbol of God, and thus male sexuality is linked not only to Christ, but in some essential way also to God.[22] But Richard Norris outlines the creedal understanding of unity in the godhead and demonstrates that even the sexuality of the man Jesus has no essential significance in the being of God.[23] It would seem as if agreement on this is possible: that while some languages assign the word God a gender, there is no sexuality — male, female, or both — inherent in the Judeo-Christian God; that any metaphoric statements which suggest such sexuality must be qualified; and that all analogical statements must be explicated in light of the theological assertion that God is beyond sexuality.

What of gender in modern American English? Anglo-Saxon, the linguistic family spoken in the British Isles in the year 1000, was an inflected language with grammatical gender like its Germanic antecedents. Into Anglo-Saxon came the Christian God, talked of in masculine gender, so translated from the Christian parent languages. Through the centuries English has become a less and less inflected language. We have now only vestiges of the old system of declining nouns and pronouns and conjugating verbs. One grammatical variable which has been almost completely abandoned is gender. Nouns no longer are arbitrarily assigned to categories called gender which influence pronoun selection and verb endings through rules of agreement. Modern American English functions almost totally with what grammarians call natural gender. That is, an animate female is "she," an animate male is "he," and all singular else is "it."

Language guidelines of publishing houses, especially those houses which produce children's books and texts, indicate the state of the language with regard to gender. Of course such thorough-going alterations of the gender system are not already commonplace in America. But we see a movement, legislated in some significant places, further to remove gender consideration in American English. The guidelines of publishers like Macmillan and McGraw-Hill make the following policies:[24] "man" and its compounds are no longer acceptable as generic terms; words like ship and country are "it," not "she"; occupations are not to be typecast by sex; occupational titles must not be sex-specific (except for sperm-donor and wet-nurse!); human emotions and manners of behavior are not to be stereotyped by sex; female gender word forms (poetess) are to be abandoned. These guidelines say of the "generic he" that it is no longer acceptable; the sentence can be reworded or cast into

---

[22] Urban T. Holmes, "The Feminine Priestly Symbol and the Meaning of God," *The Saint Luke's Journal of Theology* 17 (1974) 7.

[23] Richard A. Norris Jr., "Priesthood and the 'Maleness' of Christ: Trinity and Christology in the Fathers," *Pro and con on Ordination of Women*, Report and Papers from the Anglican-Catholic Consultation, 75-76.

[24] "Guidelines for Equal Treatment of the Sexes in the McGraw-Hill Book Company Publications," McGraw-Hill 1974; "Guidelines for Creating Positive Sexual and Racial Images in Educational Materials," Macmillan 1975; "Eliminating Stereotypes," Houghton Mifflin 1981; and "Guidelines for Improving the Images of Women in Textbooks," Scott, Foresman and Company 1974.

the plural; "he" can be replaced by "one" or "he or she" (as in "one or the other"); "he" might alternate with "she." And indication of the force of these moves is the 1977 statement by the National Council of Teachers of English, saying that except in the most strictly formal usage, "their" is preferable to "his" as a singular possessive pronoun.[25]

Perhaps the insularity of the Church has allowed this development to catch us unprepared. Are the clergy who preach about "man's salvation" aware that the children no longer define "man" to mean "human being"? Both simple and radical alterations of our speech are being called for. For example, since God is not a male being, there is no need for the word goddess. Furthermore, "masculine" and "feminine" are difficult terms, being among the most sexually stereotyped words in the language. To say that nurturing is a feminine attribute is appropriate in a discussion of Jungian archetypes, but such sexual stereotyping is not freeing to either men or women; it deepens the cultural division between women and men; and certain respectable publishing houses would find it unfit for children.

It is time to break the model of God-he. The abandonment of grammatical gender in modern American English forces religious language to alter its terminology — a move to which the Church remains lamentably resistant. If increasingly in American English "he" denotes male sexuality, it becomes a simple matter of idolatry to refer to God as "he," and this is a more seminal issue than the desire to balance male with female imagery or to ascribe to God a full range of human characteristics. English-speaking linguists have long proposed options of nonsex-specific pronouns, from Charles Converse's coinage "thon" of 1859 to the contemporary suggestion of "tey-ter-tem" for subjective, possessive, and objective cases.[26] But such a pronoun change, although attractive, is unlikely in the near future, and theologians and church people are seldom in a position to effect such a change. Even granting such a change, as in the dropping of thou-thy-thee, we need a plan for the present. Let us review the options, which unfortunately are few.

The Judeo-Christian tradition of God's not being "it" is focal, and while Dionysius called the Godhead "it" with moving awe, we do not propose to refer to God as "it." "It" is used for human persons only for infants and dead bodies, and nothing suggests that "it" will be used as a nonsex-specific personal pronoun in the future.

The third singular pronoun is "she." Some people are urging that "she," which includes the word "he," be used as the generic pronoun. (It is painfully clear that the sexual connotation of any generic pronoun is of high significance, when one hears how readily this suggestion is dismissed out of hand.) If "she" were to become a generic pronoun, God would be named "she." But this is highly unlikely.

From various corners comes the suggestion that especially God the Spirit be called "she."[27] In Hebrew, spirit, *ruah*, is feminine, and some see in the Spirit's nature

---

[25] Alleen Pace Nilsen, et al, *Sexism and Language* (Urban, Illinois: National Council of Teachers of English 1977).

[26] Casey Miller and Kate Swift, *Words and Women: New Language in New Time* (Garden City, New York: Doubleday, Anchor 1977) 116-119.

[27] For example, Jay G. Williams, "Yahweh, Women, and the Trinity," *Theology Today* 32 (1975) 240.

stereotypically feminine characteristics. But any use of "she" for God ought not be saved exclusively for God the Spirit. Assigning "he" to two persons of the Trinity and "she" to the third only further entrenches the notion of God as a sexual being. God the Spirit as "she" is unacceptable not because our God ends up only one-third female, but because we must speak of God with the highest accuracy possible, and God is neither, as modern American English knows them, he or she.

Yet there are occasions when "she" can be used metaphorically in the naming of God. Use of "she" immediately indicates the inadequacy of "he." Such metaphors occur most easily in the images of hymnody or in the extended conceits of a homily. God the Spirit might be "she" more often than God the Son, although our tradition offers examples of the Son as Lady Wisdom and Mother Church. The appositives are already in use; we need only to extend the image to include the pronoun. Furthermore, faithfulness to God as Jesus' Abba, recital of the trinitarian creeds, and reverence to Mary as Mother of God do not imply that the first person of the Trinity is not also the mother of the faithful and the mother of creation (two very different things). However, alternate use of "he" and "she" for God in metaphoric constructions is only a partial solution, and such language always requires the Aquinas test of contradictibility; God is not he, God is not she. Formal theological writing would be obscured further than it already is by an arbitrary alternation of pronouns. After all, a pronoun is meant to be a silent, unseen shorthand. Only recognition of our sexist pronoun structure forces us to focus on pronouns at all.

About the pronoun "they": contemporary grammarians realize that "they" is used regularly in spoken language as a singular generic pronoun. Some predict, even advocate, that "they" receive official singular sanction.[28] However, even if such a linguistic change would occur, "they" would not be an acceptable pronoun for God. Granting that in the Hebrew tradition one name for God, Elohim, is plural, that plural name was assigned singular meaning. The historic stress in the Judeo-Christian tradition on monotheism forces us to reject any pronoun which connotes God as plural.

Dismissing "it" and "they," awaiting "tey," and alternating "he" with "she" is hardly a happy solution. It is incumbent upon us to eliminate altogether in American English the expository use of pronouns referring to God. A growing number of Christians for whom this is a matter of conscience regularly write and speak of God without ever using masculine pronouns. Their lectures are not clumsy nor their writings awkward. They testify that it does not take long to learn to speak and write of God without such pronoun references and that the audience remains unaware of the change. As with any translation, one cannot merely substitute one word for another. Sentences must be recast. The adjective "divine" is helpful in possessive constructions. "Godself" works well as a reflexive.[29] Its initial strangeness only adds a healthy awe in speaking of God and a refusal to picture God as a superperson.

The issue is not whether one can speak and write with ease and clarity without

---

[28] Ann Bodine, "Androcentrism in Prescriptive Grammar: singular 'they,' sex-indefinite 'he,' and 'he or she,'" *Language in Society* 4 (1975) 141.

[29] For example, James F. White, *Introduction to Christian Worship* (Nashville: Abingdon 1980) 12, 18, passim.

calling God "he." There is ample and eloquent proof that such is possible. Rather, far too many theologians and church people refuse to take the matter seriously and make no attempt whatsoever to alter their speech. One would not mind occasional slips and would welcome a metaphoric use of "he" and "she" if there was evidence that the church was working against imaging God as male. As a result of the Black Power movement, educated Americans removed forthwith from their active vocabularies the word "Negro." Such alterations are quite possible if the motivation is present.

What is required is not only the will to change one's vocabulary, but a renewed perception of God. If we continue to think of human occupations as stereotypically male or female, then we must fight against our inclination to call a mailman "he" and a nurse "she." But when we think of human occupations as nonsex-specific, then mailcarriers and nurses are released from the categories of sex. If we again meet the God of the burning bush, the God of the parting waters and the raining manna, the God of the wings — the mother eagle teaching her young to fly, the mother hen protecting her chicks — the God of the cross, we might be so overwhelmed by God that we laugh at the inadequacy of "he" and resolve to be more articulate in our speech. Change of speech is a willing task if it follows a conversion of mind.

The matter of translating the Bible and theological works is more difficult than the renewal of one's own speech. Of course, biblical translations must be accurate translations of the original language. But the implications of "translation" are not self-evident. How much the original concepts require translation, especially for lectionary reading, is a highly complex question. Concepts like outdated measurements — a league, a span – are usually granted contemporary substitutions without objection, but on more sensitive issues we cannot agree as to what all constitutes translation. During the next decades as some consensus in this matter is being reached, at least we can all be responsible for our own speech, and so testify both to our intent and to our understanding of how language in America functions. Meanwhile sympathetic linguists ought to proceed with the massive task of retranslating the classic library of Christian theology. Contemporarily accurate translation of theological works will rid the study of Christianity of much of its overwhelming male overtone.

Fortunately one genre is remarkably free from the difficulty of God-he, and that is the genre of public prayer. Liturgy, since it is in the main direct address to God, has few of the third person pronouns which cause us concern. The archaic Thou-Thy-Thee has been to a great extent replaced by you-your-you, and so at least direct address to God now speaks in modern American English. So let this be our comfort: that if we are tongue-tied in preaching, speaking, and writing, we need not be so tongue-tied in praying. But our search for a new way to speak and write makes more and more attractive the Hebraic circumlocutions for the name of God. Perhaps in the end we all will agree to write in the place of God's name only four dots and to speak for the name of God only the monk's silence.

Propositions in conclusion

1 Anthropomorphism, to the extent that it is used in the description of and naming of God, should be recognized as metaphor and must be explicated with poetic sensitivity. We should balance male with female imagery, as well as use objectification and recall the *via negativa*.

2 Human relationship terms, to the extent that they are used in the description of and naming of God, should be recognized as analogical language and must be explicated with theological sensitivity in which the revelation establishes the definition.

3 The naming of the Christian God requires a paradoxical use of human language. Human models are broken by the kerygma of the cross.

4 Masculine or feminine language used in the description of and naming of God must never imply or defend male or female sexuality in the being of God. Use of "person," as in the three persons or in God as person, must never imply inherent sexuality.

5 Modern American English is moving toward a total replacement of grammatical gender with natural gender. This is, increasingly, gender equals sexuality. To the extent that this is true, expository prose cannot refer to God as he.

Language and the Aesthetic Vision

Sarah Bentley

"What follows is the spoken part of an 'informance' given at the COCU consultation on language and worship. These comments were interspersed with dances, demonstrations of forms, and movement experiences involving those present."

Introduction

As you watch these dances, keep in mind three questions: what did you *notice* most keenly; what do you *remember* (what do you see in your mind's eye or connect to in other memory-linked ways); and what do you *feel* (especially in bodily sensations)? The answers to those questions constitute the data of experience from which to draw your own conclusions about the use of movement as a language in worship.

We need to recover this language today. The basic vocabulary of sacred dance — the gestures and movements — are from the most ancient of traditions. They form a sort of *core kinesthetic speech* that is found in almost all religious dance. The key movements/postures are: standing, invoking; processing/moving toward; whirling; stomping/beating the ground with the feet; and retreating/recessing.

The Body as Instrument of Meaning

We begin with a most simple observation about the means used in speaking this language: here it is — my body. All in all it's a bit disappointing in its self-evident limitation. Take my foot — it's solid and strong, with a rather mundane quality — a good "peasant" foot. It speaks my truth for me: I'm certainly not a ballerina or a fairy princess!

This instrument — the body — reveals the type of truths I learn while working in sacred dance. Some of these meanings come to me as I observe other dancers and others come to me in my ongoing work with persons in worship and other religious settings.

First, I'm alive and I'm not perfect. The constant presentation to myself and others of this very real body reminds me that I'm on the Way, from birth to death — a finite human being.

Second, I'm strong and female. Currently some might label this an experience of androgyny — the integration of two elements usually seen as separate or opposing one another. Again, this physical truth and its expression of my (very often) strenuous and passionate dancing helps me into the reality of such statements as "Behold I am doing a new thing" (Jeremiah 31). What I affirm with my mind takes on new meaning as I struggle with my own and others' perceptions of who we each are as particular, embodied women and men.

We have spoken here of how our present language might anticipate — here and now — the final gathering, the eschatological community. As a language form, dance naturally participates in such a visioning. Watch people struggle to move, to leap, to *feel* that freedom. It is clear that we are — in all our shapes, sizes, spirits, and abilities

— showing forth the gathered community right now. That vision, which is the key motivating force behind our search for new language, is real in moments of shared and fragile humanity as we dance our lives together.

A final realization that emerges from sacred dance is our oneness with all peoples. Movement and dance are a truly universal language. Without this speech form, therefore, we are seriously limited in our ability to communicate with brothers and sisters around the globe.

The Tradition of Dance in the Church

Tradition literally means the "handing over" of a set of beliefs, teachings, attitudes toward life in this world. Here is a different mode of handing over, because dance is given and received kinesthetically — that is, through bodily sensation, especially the experience of movement within oneself. This is why dance so often surprises us with the unexpected. We perceive it in a deep and mysterious way that can only partially be known and articulated.

I am constantly discovering the traditions of sacred dance not only by reading about them, but also through traces of their language in much of the dance I see. For instance, during a recent performance in New York by Beverly Brown's company, the movement themes combined in ways that began to impress me deeply. Suddenly I realized I was remembering one of the most powerful traditions – the *dance macabre* — with its themes of denial, suffering, and death. The rich and powerful vocabulary of this tradition evoked its reponse in me despite my ignorance of it experientially. I "heard" the language spoken to me as a participant-observer and thus could know something of its meaning for the individuals and communities involved.

Another example: throughout the world culture of dance there is a tradition of androgynous figures, usually solitary, who express the rare integration of what each society may deem to be "masculine" and "feminine" traits. The older or "wisdom" figure (male or female) may have this quality and a solitary individual (a "virgin") may represent the community of both genders in dancing their life themes. A man may dance the role of a woman, or vice versa.

I knew little of this tradition when I had a startling experience watching dancer-choreographer Henry Smith perform a small segment of a piece in which an elderly wizened woman, once a great beauty, talks of losing all her loves. The transformation of this muscular man into a convincing, deeply moving female figure was effected kinesthetically, through his movement and my senses. I shook my head afterwards with the realization of how completely I was taken into this new reality, much as the rapid shift of character in Kabuki theater dissolves and reforms one's experience of male and female figures.

The tradition of morality stories — using dance or movement to depict a truth about human conduct and its consequences — similarly finds life through such contemporary works as Paul Taylor's "House of Cards," an enigmatic and at the same time oddly instructive statement about the temporal character of human existence.

Of course, the earliest origins of sacred dance traditions are in what Western educated folk persist in calling "primitive" dance — a misnomer indeed, when the same language is used in such significant and sophisticated works as Taylor's "Runes" (echoing wisdom cults of Celtic and Greek roots); Martha Graham's famous "Lamentation" (a contemporary expression with the same powerful dynamic as that at the heart of Greek tragedy and ritual); and "Esplanade," Taylor's high-energy depiction of the play-dance found the world over. Such basic and "primitive" movement may in fact account for the power of such successful dances. Increasingly, the raw or "gut" quality of such movement educates us to appreciate its earlier roots in African, Native American, and other living traditions.

Criteria and Excellence in Dance

Because dance is transmitted — given and received — kinesthetically, the question of criteria of assessment is a difficult one. I'd say good dance *moves* you — that is, it evokes some perceivable response. This can mean it disturbs, causes a subtle shuddering, or even some profound release. In this it may be interacting with and restoring memory, for we know that all experience, consciously expressed or not, remains within the somatic (bodily) realm of the individual's reality.

Movement may "hum" within us, too — I venture to say it's producing a sense of joy, exhilaration, or quiet peace — the general experience of being touched or somehow stirred tells us this is "good" dance. Within religious life this may at first cause some qualms, for Western culture (until the advent of modern dance) increasingly saw the role of dance as recreating harmony. "Beauty" in dance meant precisely that which did *not* arouse, bestir, offend — and this of course truncated the vast range of human emotions which give rise to the impulse to dance. A tendency toward this view of dance persists today.

The Healing Role of Dance

Such issues naturally suggest that dance and movement have a powerful function to play in public life. I perceive this to be a therapeutic role, for there is always at least the potential that ritual will effect healing: the exchange of truth-about-reality between participants in a living community. Thus dance may cross over (thereby integrating) the boundary between the realms of public and private, religious, and psychoanalytic practice. In so doing, it may reclaim for us all the meaning of faith at a much deeper level than is generally the case in contemporary worship. An example of this in my own work is the profound effect of repeatedly following the path of the labyrinth or maze which is set in the chancel floor in Riverside Church. A copy of the one in Chartres Cathedral, this pattern symbolizes the voyage of the soul toward union with God and was in fact the motif of many dances, ancient and medieval, in which whole communities sought deeper communion with the mystical journey of faith toward the Divine.

Like all arts, dance may restore vision to an individual and a community by reawakening the imagination. New challenges (and fresh responses to old ones) arise unexpectedly in the making and realization of a dance. In fact, dance is *another form of knowing* — capable of transcending the usual limits of our narrow and often technical reason (Tillich).

Exploring the use of dance may enrich the life of a community by demonstrating the complementarity of gifts. Not all are called to lead in or perform solo dances, but surely the whole people may be called to embody their life as a prophetic community filled with ministering souls, person with gifts to give. In this sense, dance may also lend insight to "issues" of power as well as the human vulnerability I spoke of earlier. (In fact, in the long history of dance in the Christian Church, who was allowed to dance, and where and when, often did express some clear delineations of authority wihin the community — with a marked tendency to exclude more and more folk until only bishops danced, only on special occasions, only in private!)

Overall, the *bold* use of dance may show us the Christ in new ways and help us to claim our own humanness in all aspects of life — child, adolescent, older person, wounded or dying, and so on. Physically engaging the space and symbols of the Church will give us a new sense of their meaning — both through the bodies themselves and also through the nature of the movement, provided it is clear, communicative, and compelling.

Technique and Teaching

Because of this enormous potential therefore, dance should neither be sentimentalized in its theology nor trite. It should not be based on simplistic ideas "translated" into movement. Rather it should draw on discovered (and recovered) gestures and movements with real meaning (kinesthetic resonance) in the worshipping community. This is the area of real exploration of contemporary sacred dance, as approached by people like Judith Rock and her Berkeley-based company, Body and Soul. Rock's solo, "Baptism," may leave doctrine too far behind for some viewers, while others will find it truly evocative of the soul-moving power of conversation and initiation.

The question of technique — which to use, how much attention to give it — is a hard one. It's important to see all kinds of dance, to work with many traditions. We can learn from all of them and each also has distinct limitation. The real test may be the critique of the material itself and, ultimately, the integrity of the experience for the dancer and the congregation.

For me, some modern techniques do not adequately convey the raw power of much religious and biblical material. I need less "uplift" and more sheer drive and energy. For this reason, the dominant imposition of ideals and standards from both ballet and modern dance may be a limitation to the communicative power of sacred dance. Why? Because dance is part of a whole. Our experience of it is fed and sustained by all that surrounds it and the attitudes and values expressed in certain techniques simply do not fill out the range of expression demanded by sacred dance.

Is Dance Sacred? Is It A Vocation?

It's important to note that such criticism as I am making here depends on a view that sacred dance interacts vitally with everyday life. Just as worship is not wholly out of the "usual" space and time, the music and costumes, themes, and movement of sacred dance may creatively be used to express continuity with, and not alienation from, everyday life.

Here I express profound debt to the Native American tradition, as well as Jewish cultural movements and the contemporary rediscovery of worship by feminists and goddess-seekers. These faith communities lend the following insights about the nature of sacred dance.

It is never found in a vacuum, separate from the lives and struggles of a real community. It is not done by paid performers on a stage (thus subtly transformed in a commodity for purchase). It is not given to the young and beautiful alone; rather all members of the community at one time or another may participate in and understand the reality of this language. Finally, it is practiced to invoke and release *power*, in order to serve the purposes of the community, to keep alive the spirit. Thus in these cultures, dance may express the ultimate in shared authority: graceful humility before God and others.

Is There Such A Thing as "Christian Dance"?

I think here of the "unity" prayer in John 17: "That all may be one." As I have said, the universality of dance suggests that the eschatological reality is present: all *are* one, the world already is united. The presence of spiritually-rooted persons such as Toby Towson (a Sufi) in the world of dance performers has raised questions for me about the validity of claiming uniqueness for Christian dance *per se*. But it is true that we may dance within our own tradition in ways that incorporate our particular witness, history, and ministry.

This will be true for individuals as well. For instance, these were my dances and reflected my experiences of my body in the world, in relationship to others and to my faith. I grew up sitting still in church, next to a rather unexpressive father who scowled at children who moved during the service! I also went to church seeking a deep connection, spiritual as well as physical, to others and to the nurturing presence I had lost with my mother's death. Before that I came from generations of Methodists who practiced strict adherence to disciplines, became prosperous, and clung to sterile notions of "high" art and music — no excess here, thank you! I came too from farm people who couldn't verbalize a great deal and were somewhat embarrassed by show of beauty, sensuality, or eccentricity. Mixed in with these heritages are the peculiar sorrows and joys of the individuals who formed my immediate family. Consequently, I am the sum of all these memory-experiences and in some way they have all made me who I am as a dancer.

Power and Vulnerability

This discussion, unexpectedly, has brought me back to theology, or specifically to my older heritage, Perfectionism. Let me reiterate what I continue to learn in movement and dance about all that. First, as I said, there is the Reality we call the Body. Mine is anything but Ideal. I deal with that every time I stand up in public. Also, I make a lot of mistakes in dancing. My impatience with myself only interferes with the implicit sense of timing that somehow, miraculously appears when I least expect it. The process of learning tolerance and respect for myself and others tells me more about *becoming* than any philosophical speculation.

Second, the future *is* always open: the unexpected is always present in doing and seeing dance. "Where will this movement go?" "How do you know when to end?" "Where did THAT image come from?!" I am continually amazed at the learning that goes on for me and other people as we let down into this creative process and allow ourselves to be surprised by what happens to us together.

Third, I have a new sense of the claim that *actions constitute persons and community.* Slowly I realize that if I don't dance, I will not, in some mysterious way, be myself — perhaps as a result I may cause the community to be diminshed. If I don't use my body and use it well, my spirit suffers. If I don't show my vulnerability as well as my strength, I may in fact be less powerful. And if I don't reveal myself, I am, in the end, not able to be with you.

We have only touched on such things in this consultation, by noting the connection between language and control. In some way, all I have said is about such questions in my life and, I imagine, in yours. In dance I must constantly seek loss of old ideas or preconceptions, previous experiences of control — in order to gain new power and effectiveness. I must strive for a diminishing of manipulation both in the allowing of my own dances and the evoking of yours. In all this we hope together for a restoration of the grace which we claim is the mark of our redemption.

Dance As Witness: An Ideal Speech?

So I dance . . . and invite you to find your own dancing as well. This is for me some sort of imperative — at least in the exploring. For, if *we* don't dance, we may abrogate the power to evoke more of Life in this world. If *I* don't, I may reject creation as good (a somewhat morbid tendency all-too-familiar within the Christian tradition, according to Frankie Schaeffer in his little book entitled, *Addicted to Mediocrity*).

Without some really live physical experience in worship, I fear we worship falsely, praising God with one hand — and denying him/her with our other. Is it a sin not to dance? If you're feeling a bit uneasy or irritated at this point, I'm not taking it that far! I would say we are about correcting a deep imbalance, in fact a kind of injustice. For surely it's unjust not to nurture life — in its deepest, expressive forms — until the end of our life on this earth. For me, movement and dance may go some way toward overcoming the powerful repression of feeling and of physical expressiveness in general that has characterized much of the Western and Eastern religious tradition. We are the people who preach that "the word of God in history is *Love*" and believe in Jesus Christ *incarnate* and ourselves as the *Body* of Christ in the world. With such a tradition, and surrounded as we are by so much bitterness, death and capitalization on the dire needs and fears of all people — how can we NOT show forth our faith in any living form possible, including movement and dance?! And by so doing, we may be — *we are already* — part of an ancient and universal tradition, instruments of peace and healing in the world.

A Moving Blessing

You see, I am alive.
I stand in good relation to the gods.
I stand in good relation to all that is beautiful.
I stand in good relation to you.
You see, I am alive.
I am alive.

        Navajo

Seminars

The Power of Language in Preaching *

Ann G. Denham

I suppose it is a toss-up as to which I love more, words or preaching. Language, that mystery by which sound and image call forth feeling and meaning, bind time and identity, skate along the edge of possibility, and, occasionally, open out into an unknown dimension.

Preaching, that enfleshing of Spirit, wedding of God's Word to human made symbols, witnessing to the power of each, incarnating the one — God's Word — in homily happenings, but never reducing it to them. Presenting the other — words — as the identical tools with which we order a Big Mac, yet, ever so often nudging those words askew, revealing their unexpected doorway into depths, if we have the courage to enter.

Writing a sermon is like making a good soup. The words and images which pass through the head and heart, as the scripture is mulled and pondered, enrich the broth and flavor the mix, even when they lose their identity and are never mentioned by name.

I am a peripatetic preacher. (I've always wanted to use that word.) As the perennial guest in the pulpit, I always start fresh, can never assume, never build. For me the twenty-minute sermon is as exacting an art form as the villanelle.

I hope to do a couple of things. First, I want to convince you of the power — the unbelievable depth of power — of words, language. Second, I want to share the way I go about tapping and harnessing that power in preaching, which, for me is at bottom, the creation of a world and the enabling of persons to enter.

Language is really what separates us from other animals. So called higher animals can solve problems, use tools and employ sounds as signals. Chimpanzees have even been taught to communicate with letters and blocks. But no other animal establishes a world by naming it and thereby calling it forth from what otherwise would be a chaotic mass of sense perceptions.

Annie Sullivan says of Helen Keller, "If I can just teach her one word, I can unlock her world." It is in learning that everything has a name, in making the connection between the finger symbols for water and the cool wet stuff flowing from the pump, that the world of objects and ideas opens to Helen. To have the word is to possess the power to call forth worlds. "Open Sesame" is more than superstition. Even our modern courts recognize the power of libel or "fighting words." And one is not free to shout "Fire!" in a crowded theatre.

Language is what enables us to interpret and organize the world we experience through our senses. It provides structure to what would otherwise be just a jumble of impressions. The other side of that is that language limits the thinking of its speakers. It serves as a filter to screen reality. We once believed that our perceptions, our seeing, hearing, feeling, and so on, were simply reactions to impingements on them by the world "out there." We thought our perceptions then sent these outside messages to the brain, where we put together a reasonable facsimile of what *was* out there. We nov know that our concepts, our basic assumptions, actively direct our perceptions. We

* Quotations from *The Origin of Consciousness in the Breakdown of the Bicameral Mind*, by Julian Jaynes, Copyright © 1976 by Julian Jaynes, reprinted by permission, Houghton-Mifflin Company.

see and feel and hear according to what Brunner calls a selective program of the mind. What we are conditioned to find out there is what we find. There is no way of escaping this rich web of language, myth, history and ways of doing things so unconsciously accepted that they go without saying and make up our only reality. This inherited worldview is largely a language-made affair.

Example: English, whose speakers live mainly in temperate zones, has one word for snow. The Aztec had one word, and they used it for snow and cold and hail and ice and anything cold. In a subtropical zone, it didn't come up very often. The Avilik Eskimo, who live above the Arctic Circle, have over 50 words for snow. Different words for snow falling, snow on the ground, snow blowing in the wind, snow mixed with sleet, snow packed for building blocks. Their awareness of the different aspects of snow, ice, wind, and ground and the shifting relationships among them — awareness grounded in language — makes it possible for the Avilik Eskimo to travel freely under conditions that would mean certain death to anyone else. Anthropologist Edmund Carpenter writes of travelling by dog sled where there is no line dividing earth from sky, no perspective, an all-white world, a land without bottom or edge. Yet they travel it and are seldom lost. Says Carpenter, I looked at the utter sameness of the earth and could not imagine what reference points the driver was using. Minute perceptions, anchored in vocabulary, enable the Avilik Eskimo to navigate the Arctic wastes.

Now this may sound simple enough, but let it really sink in. What you have in your head affects what is out there for you. And it may be a matter of life and death.

Let me bring it closer to home with a personal story. Several years ago, I officiated at a garden wedding. Through a chain of circumstances, I arrived later than I had planned and a number of guests were presenting themselves at the front door. I had not met the bride's parents, although they knew I was a woman. When I reached the door, robe over my arm, Book of Worship in my hand, I offered my right hand and said: "I'm Ann Denham. I'm the minister." Nothing happened. I couldn't think of a shorter way, so I again said: "I am Ann Denham. I'm the minister." Then I added: "I imagine Sue is wondering where I am." Nothing. You know how time stands still at times like this? I have to get inside. I can't think of a faster way to say it. So, once again I say: "I am Ann Denham. I'm the minister." The woman takes my hand, turns to her husband and says: "This is Ann Denham. She's from Minnesota." If you are far enough from what is expected as a "minister" you are rendered invisible. You can't be heard at all.

Words do more than communicate, they conjure images. We are not dealing with concepts which are linear and can be formulated and made precise and changed at will. We are dealing with images which, once created, have a life of their own. Images function almost without our conscious awareness. Minority children in a racist society have internalized an image of inferiority before they reach the age of conceptualizing.

An image is not a simple mistake, easily corrected. A child told she is stupid long enough, really becomes stupid. A woman told she can't lead or make decisions long enough, really loses the power to lead or decide. Definition through language and image becomes a self-fulfilling prophecy. Notions concerning men or women, members of certain races, persons of certain color come so to embody our proper perceptions of them that we say it is their nature. As any fool can plainly see, that is the way they really are.

It is tough to change language not because it is trivial and so not worth the bother, but because it strikes at the very roots of our perception of reality. We refuse to say chairperson not because it is silly or because chairman is officially correct, but because it removes the blinders from our eyes and opens possibilities which are frightening and exhausting to contemplate.

Amending the language to render it inclusive is a work of justice. For the power attendant upon language is the power of gods. In our culture the word man evokes male. (The simple fact that our word for male is also the word for everybody speaks reams.) Policeman cuts off woman's possibilities in a way that police officer does not. Simply harnessing the power of the word man — and it is the most overworked word in the English language — harnessing it for inclusiveness, is an act of justice. Cutting that word down to size, diverting its inflated power into officer, carrier, worker, member, citizen, work hours, synthetic, human energy, one to one, fill or staff. This work is not cosmetic. Personally, I have taken a vow not to read exclusive language in public. I will lector and edit or I will not lector. I once sight read all of Psalm One, mostly putting it into the plural. "You have made us a little lower than the angels." I applaud the word "herstory" in all its audacious absurdity. And I pity pedantic types who suppose feminists don't know that history comes from *histor*, meaning knowledge. We know it doesn't mean "his story." But through some magic of synchronicity, the word says what it is. And "herstory" raises our consciousness to the way most people and nearly all women are omitted from the human story.

I want to turn now to a closer look at how words function to produce images and ideas. I want to talk specifically about metaphor and about symbols.

(This discussion of metaphor is taken from Julian Jaynes, *The Origin of Consciousness in the Breakdown of the Bicameral Mind*, in some cases, word for word.)

"The most fascinating property of language is its capacity to make metaphors. Metaphor is not a sort of decoration, an extra trick, as we were taught in classes on composition. Metaphor is the very constitutive ground of language. I am using metaphor here in its most general sense: the use of one term for one thing to describe another because of some kind of similarity between them or between their relations to other things."

"It is by metaphor that the language grows. The common reply to the question 'What is it?' when a reply is difficult or an experience unique is 'Well, it is like . . . a flying saucer, with a sort of egg-beater on top.' Experiments done in laboratories with both adults and children describing nonsense objects reveal that the approach is always one of metaphor, quickly reduced to code words and labels."

"The human body has been a prolific source of metaphor, creating previously unspeakable distinctions in a host of areas. The head of an army, table, page, bed, household, or nail; or of steam or water; the face of a clock, cliff, card, or crystal; the eyes of needles, wind storms, targets, flowers, or potatoes; the brow of the hill; the cheeks of the vise; the teeth of cogs or combs; the lips of pitchers, craters, or augers; the tongues of shoes, boardjoints, or railway switches; the arm of a chair or the sea; the leg of a table, compass, sailor's voyage, or cricket field and so on and on and on."

"This is language moving out into the space of the world to describe it and perceive it more and more definitely. But language also moves in another more important way, behind our experiences on the basis of structures in our nervous systems to create abstract concepts whose referents are not observable, except in a metaphorical sense. So we speak of the nub, the heart, the pith, kernal, core, marrow of an idea, which is itself a metaphor and seen only with the mind's eye. Language and its referents have climbed up from the concrete to the abstract on the steps of metaphors."

"The concepts of science are all of this kind, abstract concepts generated by concrete metaphors. In physics we have force, acceleration (to increase one's steps), inertia (originally an indolent person), resistance, fields, and now, charm."

"Metaphor is how we understand. We arrive at a metaphor for a thing by substituting something more familiar to us. The feeling of familiarity is the feeling of understanding."

"Generations ago we would understand thunder storms as the rumbling in battle of superhuman gods. Today, we reduce the storm to various supposed experiences with friction, sparks, vacuums, and the imagination of bulgeneous banks of burly air smashing together to make noise. None of these really exist as we imagine them. Yet they act as metaphor and feel familiar and we say we understand the storm."

Get this. When Christians say the Kingdom of Heaven is a mustard seed or leaven hid in a measure of meal or that God is a father who had two sons or a woman who lost a coin or a lover who comes leaping the mountains, peeping in at the lattice, whose face is joy, when we employ metaphor, we are not up to some artsy-cutsey trick of make believe. We are interacting with reality by understanding through metaphor. This is the way we build all our realist worlds.

Let's look for a minute at how a metaphor works. There are always two terms in a metaphor and Jaynes coins words for them. There is the thing to be described, or metaphrand, and the thing used to elucidate or shed light on it, the metaphier.

Consider the metaphor that the snow blankets the ground. The metaphrand is something about the completeness and even thickness with which the ground is covered by snow. The metaphier is a blanket on a bed. But the pleasing nuances of this metaphor are the associations of blanket which Jaynes calls paraphiers. Something about warmth, protection, and slumber until some period of awakening. These associations of blanket automatically become associations of the way the snow covers the ground. And thus we have created by this metaphor the idea of the earth sleeping and protected by the snow cover until its awakening in the spring. All this is packed into the simple use of the word blanket to pertain to the way the snow covers the ground.

"Not all metaphors have such generative potential. 'The ship plows the sea' is a rather exact correspondence. But if I say, 'The brooks sing through the woods,' the similarity of the brook's bubbling and gurgling and the metaphier of, presumably, a child singing is not at all exact. It is the paraphrands of joy and dancingness becoming associated with the brook that are of interest."

"In the comparison of love to a rose, it is not the tenuous correspondence of metaphrand and metaphier, but the paraphrands which engage us. That love lives in the sun, smells sweet, has thorns when grasped and blooms for a season only."

"Or suppose I say less visually and so more profoundly something quite opposite, that my love is like a tin smith's scoop, sunk past its gleam in the meal bin. The immediate correspondence here — of being out of casual sight, is trivial. Instead it is the paraphrands of this metaphor which create what could not possibly be there, the enduring, careful shape and hidden shiningness and holdingness of a lasting love deep in the heavy, manipulable softness of mounding time, the whole simulating, and so paraphranding, sexual intercourse from a male point of view. Love has not such properties except as we generate them by metaphor." To create metaphor is to reveal more of reality through giving ourselves to the possibility of such associations.

Metaphors are powerful — and they have the advantage that they can be created at will. Symbols, which must emerge, are the most powerful components of language and are described by some as "living entities."

We think of symbols as being objects and so they are. And that is the most powerful way to experience them: water, cup, light, bread. But each symbol has a name and very powerful images can be set in motion through words functioning as symbol.

Words, of course, involve us here because they are the stuff of preaching. It is important to understand the symbolic dimension of words because the religious world view is a symbol system, its power dependent on living symbols, enfleshed in lives, bringing forth spirit to visibility in our midst.

A sign stands for content that is absent but known: a dollar sign, a billboard, a stop light. Symbols, and the words that name them, stand for a present reality, which can only be known by participation. The power is neither in the object or the subject alone. Symbols are relational. A symbol demands commitment as a condition of entrance. If you aren't willing to enter, you reduce a symbol to a sign. The result of symbolic activity is the experience of meaning. Not intellectual understanding alone, but an experience of the whole self. All symbolism is ultimately religious for it opens us up to Reality.

Victor Turner, a social anthropologist, has done a lot of work with symbols as they function in African tribal ritual. He describes three important properties that can give us a better idea of the depth and power of symbolic language.

1. Multivocality or condensation. A whole system of culture or belief may be represented in a single symbol. To offer the symbol is to open a multi-leveled world. So, in Christian symbolism there is water which is at once fertility and destruction, refreshment and drowning, the primal waters over which the Spirit hovered, the rivers of Paradise, Noah's flood, Jacob's well, the parting Red Sea, water from rock, wine from water, walking on water, baptism, foot washing, the cup of cold water, living water, and the crystal sea of Revelation. To hit the high spots.

2. Second property, ability to unite disparate signata and so to heal paradoxes. By virtue of analogy or association in fact or thought, it is possible for one symbol to condense, convey, and make intelligible combinations which cannot be successfully dealt with separately. For example, the Trinity, which unites the powerful, creating God and the powerless, suffering God, together with the transcendent-immanent God

and the just-loving God, all the while uniting time and eternity, while demonstrating that love is relational and God is a community.

3. Particularly important for Turner is polarization of meaning. He describes the two poles of a symbol: one, ideological, for the head, the other, sensory, for the heart. In ritual, the two poles are brought close to each other in a context of social excitement and discharge their energy. Raw, physical energy is ennobled by meaning. Ideals and ideas are fired by drives and urges. Let me give you an example. For the Ndembu, the musoli tree with its white sap is a sacred symbol. It is called the milk tree and represents the tribe, which traces its lineage through the mothers. At the opposite pole, it stands for mother's milk and arouses feelings about nursing and weaning, plenty and want, acceptance and rejection.

In ritual, these poles are brought close together and discharge their energy. Raw, unconscious feelings are enabled by meaning and tamed by the ideal of the community and tribal solidarity is given new energy. It is hard to examine our own symbols in this way.

One possible comparison might be the secular ritual of football. We bring our national flag onto the field and sing the national anthem and sometimes have a prayer. Then two teams of grown men, paid phenomenal wages, slam and wham and beat each other to a pulp as they compete to move a ball up and down the field in order to score. Voluptuous young women cavort on the sidelines. And the purpose of the referees is not so much to catch every infraction of the rules, as to oversee a nuanced version of fair play consonant with the desired amount of action. Is football analogous to notions by which American life is lived? If you can't get there, we'll bring it into your living room — with timely messages on the good life. "You only go around once, better grab that gusto." "Weekends belong to Michelob." "This Bud's for you, for all you do, the king of beers is coming through." I don't even watch football. I picked up all of this just calling people to dinner. Why am I singing commercials? Aside from the fact that they are the highest paid, most creative, most potent language constructions around? Well, some people who know about such things believe we are approaching the time when commercials will be our only *shared* images and language.

We've been led to believe that the symbol system of Christian faith is not really real. It's made up. Symbolic, which in this culture means substitute for the real thing (like preaching means scolding and ritual means going through the motions.) Of course it's symbolic! So is all reality. That's the only kind a symbolizing creature can have.

The problem is not as we have been led to believe, how to make symbols powerful, but how do we wake up to the power of all symbols? How do we learn to tell the ones which liberate from the ones that limit and con and destroy?

To follow Victor Turner, we bring to our fabricated reality the fears of a totally contingent creature that knows it will die. A creature that symbolizes to deaden the fear, to seek security, to locate the hurt "out there" by defining others and enemies who can then be placated or destroyed. A creature who builds idols. We bring this basic emotion into close contact with our symbol system and — voilà!, a sense of power, which we believe can save us. We will die for our symbols. We will kill for our symbols. It is, as anthropologist Ernest Becker says, not viciousness but our desperate need to make panic look reasonable that spills so much of others' blood. Roheim, an anthropologist of religions, muses that culture, a symbol system, is at bottom the fabrication of a child afraid in the dark. Well, what symbols would be appropriate to adults, who knew reality was symbolic, and who knew that they were afraid?

The necessity of commitment to the language question, of waking up to what is at stake, is as pressing as any other item on our agenda. For it may come down to "shoot out at the O.K. corral." The dialogue will be artificial, out of a grade B film. But it will be real enough to incinerate the planet.

I attended a lector workshop in which we were told of reading the Word. This is your message. You have this one chance to get it through. Announce the reading. Then wait ten years. Wait until the rustling dies down and people are attentive. You have a word that means life or death. Project, they must hear you. Enunciate and phrase, they must understand you. Know your message and concentrate on communicating it, they must believe you. Prepare and read as if everything depended on it. Because it does.

Preaching

Christians are called to root their lives in a vision of reality which the secular world has judged unreal and untrue, to give energies and priorities to persons and projects the culture has labeled impossible. There is no getting around the fact that we are called to live out of a space that is not of this world: for a kingdom, under a reign, caught up in a dimension.

The Christian answer for contingent, fearful, idol-making creatures is to be found in the story of God's dealings with Israel and in the life, death, and resurrection of Jesus Christ. This worldview is held in powerful language and images. Some are as old as the most primitive archetypes of human evolution. Some are as fresh as this morning's encounter, as believer surrenders to possibility and Spirit blows where it wills.

This worldview is held in community — women and children and men. Mary Magdalene and Peter and John and Paul; Jewish strands and Greek strands and Medieval Europe; Black and Asian and Hispanic; Pope and pauper and Puritan; the superstitious, the scholar, dissenter, preserver, renewer, ecumenist, heretic, and saint.

To preach is to stand among this company — in relationship to these symbols, incarnating the metaphors by making available the power of your person and telling the truth about the world and the reign of God, from this point of view. In short, to witness, to witness as one who was there. Hearsay is not enough.

If this sounds like an enormous task, it is. One enters the pulpit to witness to the way of this dimension — for this dimension is less a place than an orientation — and closer to improvised dancing than moving in. Like riding a bicycle, it can only be described once you are doing it. One enters the pulpit to make available the symbols which convey the possibility of entrance. The preacher must know the symbol system and live intimately with it. He had better know his Bible. She should understand doctrine, not as quaint, old-timey rules, but as descriptions of this kingdom. They had better spend time with the symbols in prayer and read and reread the stories.

But the preacher can't stop with the symbols. Preaching is never explaining, talking about, illustrating the symbols. A symbol talked about, explained, ceases to function, to lead us to depths. Definition cuts off possibility. Literal interpretation and demythologizing alike reduce a world of symbols to dead signs. The real Word is incarnate, embodied, brought to visibility, fleshed out. It is not so much built as birthed.

Because it is symbolic, the witness must be whole. When the preacher does not bring head and heart, does not open to the Word, in life, the preaching is like inviting your friends to dinner, gathering them around the table and reading them the recipes of all your favorite dishes, then adjourning to the parlor and reading them the recipe for black forest cake and continental coffee. That's not how meals are made. That's not how worlds are made. That's not how preaching is made.

There is a way of looking at Christian faith that holds that we can know more of Christ and the workings of the Spirit than even the disciples. We have the witness of the ages. And to open ourselves to the symbols is to learn something new. Not just new to us, but a new revelation. Our incarnation of Spirit brings more to light, more to visibility, brings more reality into being.

Last fall I was involved in a theology weekend for the women of our Conference. One woman raised an image I cannot forget. Speaking of the traditional words, "This is my body, broken for you" she observed: "Everyone of us is here because some woman broke her body to give us birth. Body often taking the limit of what body could bear."

What is this new slant on old words saying? Does this somehow illumine the fierce emotion surrounding women as priests or preachers? Do we fear the connection because it would reveal that breaking body for another is as common as birth? That Jesus broken on the cross was as bloodied and broken and taboo as a post-partum woman? Might this image — a woman breaking bread — add a dimension to the symbol? Lift it from magic and privileged position? "This is my body, broken for you, that you might have life."

When any person enters the pulpit to enflesh and witness to God's Word, it is always a time of possibility. And when a woman — or a minority — enters, who has been excluded, the possibility that God may do a new thing is even greater.

Sacramento Roman Catholics just ordained their first Hispanic bishop. I watched the rite on television. After he was ordained, anointed, mitred, a music group — that seemed to this Anglo a brassy night club act, guitars, horns, sequins — began to play and sing a lively song, "Amigo." And all the bishops passed by Bishop Gallegos and embraced him and gave him the kiss of peace. And I learned something I hadn't known before. Something inexpressible in "mere words." *You* didn't see and hear, so I told you, in words to help you see and hear in your mind's eye. But if I draw you a picture and explain too much about the band and the song, "Amigo" and the bishops as colleagues and the history of the kiss of peace and why I was moved, the possibility for you to enter is lost.

We are a multi-leveled people. There is more to us than meets the eye. The word must reach more than the rational ego. There must be depth that speaks to depth, succor which loosens bonds at the level of repressed memory and to depth, succor which loosens bonds at the level of repressed memory and personal unconscious; there must be gestures of trust that help us to open doors and cross thresholds. It will not do to offer three points for the head and an emotional zap for the heart. Information for the ego and a rush of emotion, simulating movement. Preaching must beckon, not sucker people in. It must be truth, not propaganda. It must be invitation, not seduction.

We use the word seduction to speak of pressuring someone less knowledgeable to surrender will and judgment to another whose motivation and intentions are questionable. In particular, we use this word to describe breaking down defenses and gaining access to the deepest center of another. The preacher can simulate movement with a guilt trip or a long, sad story. We all know buzz words and frightening words and rally-around words. You can make some people believe they are moved with a stained-glass voice. Preaching respects the integrity of symbols and of hearers. It must not be manipulation but invitation to surrender.

The preacher presents the symbol — the worldview, testifies that it is of God (Word of God) and can be trusted. She invites the hearers to enter, to give themselves, to surrender. What is offered must not be false promises but true Gospel – tested and attested in the history and present life of God's people; tested and attested in the life of the preacher.

More truth is revealed as we are open to and embody the symbol in its depth, incarnating Spirit in our lives, individually and as a community. We hold the symbol reciprocally, we call each other on testing and entering and surrendering. Some will be wrong, but not all will be. Our mutual experience gives depth, richness and possibility. Holding to the tradition, skating at the edges of language, pushing out the boundaries of possibility, in order to actualize more and more.

Sometimes I get scared and turn back. The process of incarnation and surrender is costly. It is putting the center of our lives, moment by moment, at the disposal of what we say we believe, enfleshing the impossible in our person. Consenting again and again to transfiguration. Dying and being reborn.

Sometimes the preacher can only confess he is unable to enter. Sometimes the preacher can only bring on the scene the Word, the witness of the church, and her own fears and share the wrestling. One word, touched with genuine life struggle, can be a rock in the desert. A language palace built on *Reader's Digest* platitudes won't shelter you through the closing hymn.

What must not happen is reduction of the Word to something less; bringing it to equation with some empty notion, hypocritically pretending it is something "higher." The common, the ordinary is vehicle for this living Word, but not identical with it. This kind of reduction is very common; salvation reduced to a balanced personality; agape to extroversion and folksiness; the victory of Christ to choosing sides in a revolution. Thomas Merton says this is because we don't really want "the Kingdom" but something of our own making. He even suggests we might change "Thy Kingdom come" to "give us more time."

I want you to get this. As Peggy Way once said, "This is real stuff." This is the realest thing I know, birthing sermons. But the process talked about turns flat. The words spill out and lie there. I want you to get it!

How can we get it? This is the crux of all preaching. As the preacher sits there, winding up metaphors, ducking into symbols, hoping to come out unscathed. How can this word — often in images we have worn smooth — how can this word explode in us in that instantaneous association-reaction we call "getting it"? That miracle binding of mind and body, that glorious happening we call the laugh — or the a-ha! Let me close by sharing the creation of a sermon, a feminist sermon.

You can't explain a sermon either, but I preached last Christmas on "getting it." I can't take credit, it fell into my head from the Spirit. The text was Matthew's "This is how the birth of Jesus Christ came about," angels, prophetic dreams, Spirit visitations. If we're going to get it, set these aside. Look for the in-group assumptions. What Matthew's readers didn't even know they knew. That's where a joke dwells. *This* is how the birth of Jesus Christ came about. Ann and Joachim were about to unload a daughter. Then carefully-worded stuff on position of women in First Century Palestine. There is an impediment — it can't be fixed up with more dowry — Mary is with child. This is a scandal you don't live down in a generation. Adultery! Description of the only trial by ordeal in the Bible. The woman forced to undergo it in the temple. If guilty, execution by stoning or burning alive. What went without saying — the existential situation of Mary's yes. The graphic description skates the edge of merely horrifying, so pull it back. Harness it — with words. "But don't get hung up on the hideous process of a patriarchy controlling paternity. Let the horror open out on every attempt to suppress and crush. All systems where the powerful exact a perfection from the powerless they would never ask of themselves. Let it open out on all misguided forms of redemption through hatred and force, making the world good with punishment and pain."

Contrast with incarnation of perfect love, a deity who takes on flesh to be with his people, bears their barbaric punishments.

Back to the punch line: this is how the birth of Jesus Christ came about. Before her marriage, Mary, his mother, was found to be with child. Genealogy — five women in Jesus' family tree. Who? Rachel? Sarah? No. Rahab, a prostitute; Ruth, who tricked a man into marrying her; Tamar, who played the harlot with her father-in-law; Bathsheba, who committed adultery with King David. And, of course, Mary, who was found to be with child before her marraige. What kind of Messiah sets five shady ladies in his family tree? One who reforms by loving, defuses death by dying. Harlots and tax collectors go into his Kingdom before priests and levites.

Nelle Morton's stuff on First Century Palestine — men, women, children; boy child more important than girl child. Only one human creature lower than a girl child, an illegitimate boy. No name, no father, no lineage. A girl could marry into a name. A bastard boy, never. In this the Messiah, the lowest of the low, can find a place.

Keep coming back to "This is how the birth of Jesus Christ came about." Show how those words reveal things we never expected. At the end, bring back the dream, the angels. This is no airy, fairy tale, but the poverty of human imagination in the presence of what really happened. "Bring back the angel. Make it a chorus, hovering on wings of gold. Set them in a sky that is at once the clearest starry night and the most glorious sunrise you have ever known. Add an exploding nova, a rare conjunction of planets. Call in the magi — the wise ones. I favor an even dozen, assorted colors and races and ages, half of them female. Look for animals kneeling in the University farm and weird reactions in your laboratory cultures. Bring out everything that sings out the power and glory and love of God — and set it alongside that outcast, shivering mite — who is nevertheless God-with-us and we will only have begun to 'Get it.' This is how the birth of Jesus Christ came about. Before her marriage, Mary, his mother, was found to be with child, through the power of the Holy Spirit."

The hearers at that Newman Center at U.C. Davis who were willing to follow me deeper and deeper into the words "this is how the birth of Jesus Christ came about" tell me that something new exploded in them. And I know that when I followed the lead of the Spirit, writing the sermon in about an hour, I "saw" more and more as I moved with excitement and trembling. It seemed as though I had spent a lifetime enfleshing those symbols and learning those bits of information for just that time of connection and revelation.

Only to give it up, of course. It happens again and again, if we are faithful. New seeing, breaking camp, forsaking idols, stepping out in trust, dying to transformation, receiving our new name. Again and again, until we catch the rhythm. Or dig in our heels and in fear and despair, refuse to dance. There is here no lasting city. The place of transformation cannot be known until we get there. We must work in the dark, in the depths of symbol and image, where we cannot really know what we are doing.

Bibliography:

Words and Women: New Language in New Times, Casey Miller and Kate Swift. Anchor Press/Doubleday, Garden City, New York, 1976.

The Crack in the Cosmic Egg: Challenging Constructs of Mind and Reality, Joseph Chilton Pearce. Pocket Book Edition, New York, 1974.

Origin of Consciousness in the Breakdown of the Bicameral Mind, Julian Jaynes. Houghton, Mifflin Co., Boston, 1976.

The Truth is Concrete, Dorothee Soelle. Herder and Herder, New York, 1969.

The Ritual Process, Victor Turner. Cornell Paper Backs, Ithaca, New York, 1977.

Dramas, Fields and Metaphors, Victor Turner. Cornell University Press, Ithaca and London, 1974.

"Preaching the Word" by Nell Morton in *Sexist Religion and Women in the Church*, edited by Alice L. Hageman, Association Press, New York, 1974.

Words That Hurt: Language and Justice

James F. White

As Christians, we are unable to be indifferent to issues of justice. The worship of the Church and all its other activities are deeply involved in concerns about justice. Without proper care, these activities can promote justice or thwart it. For our purposes here, we shall define justice as rendering to each person his or her due by attributing to each person full human worth. Language is a most basic element in forming people to express justice. For example, it is impossible to use such terms as "nigger," "wop," "fairy," etc. without implying that a person is due less than full human worth. Not only does the use of such terms reveal unjust attitudes but it also creates and reinforces attitudes and behavior inimical to justice. On this basis, one cannot say "it is only words" but rather must say "it is nothing less than words."

Words can hurt very deeply, especially when they imply that another being or group of beings are due less human worth than others. Words can demean and oppress others in ways that can be very painful to those victimized by them. But those using such language are themselves deprived in that consciously or unconsciously they are denying the Christian imperatives to deal justly with others. Thus a continuing process of education is necessary to make us all aware of what language does to us as well as for us. Only by becoming sensitive can we avoid the use of words that hurt.

There are many other ways in which worship expresses injustices beyond the use of words. Roles people play such as ushers, garb worn such as preaching robes with padded shoulders, the Christian calendar itself, all these are examples of actions that reveal discriminatory attitudes. The reticence of many churches to have a prominent baptismal font (perhaps the most female symbol the Church has) is simply a symptom of a prejudice we may not recognize until confronted by it. The wedding service has traditionally implied subservience on the part of the woman. Our action and our words are inextricably mixed but they reveal similar attitudes. Fortunately, we can analyze words with more ease since they can all be written down on paper and examined. But ultimately, our words and actions are one. We shall limit ourselves here to words since they are easier to analyze although we must always remember their linkage to action. We shall look first at language about humans and then see how such language shapes our language about God.

I

Much of our society has acknowledged rapid change in language about humans. Of course, change in language is nothing new. In the fourteenth century, Chaucer remarked on how "in forme of speche is chaunge" and words that once had meaning, but now seem strange to us, people once used "and spedde as wel in love as men now do." Words such as "men, mankind, man" no longer mean in American English what they did ten years ago. A decade ago they referred to all humans, today they mean half the human race. The scandal, of course, is that we were not aware of how unjust it was to equate maleness with normative humanity. Our language implied that femaleness was derivative and less than fully human. It is now widely realized that such language is morally wrong and must be rejected. Much of this recognition has come outside the Church yet the Church dare not lag behind movements for justice in society. Hence school children are no longer taught the generic use of terms such as "man" and many editors now reject such usage in publications.

It is important to recognize that these changes in human language have preceded those in God language. But they have also made changes in God language inevitable.

Many problems occur in biblical translation. In many cases, terms such as "if any man" have been used when the meaning is clearly "if anyone." Thus much gratuitous male language has been supplied by translators when it is not found in the biblical languages themselves. Furthermore, in Greek, the pronoun is often a part of the verb. Many pronouns, usually of a male gender, have been introduced by the translators. Thus much gender-exclusive language for both humans and God is not in the texts.

Our position is the need to be faithful to the original biblical texts. One does not have the right to rewrite scripture; one often has the responsibility to retranslate it. Certainly the biblical world was male dominated and this is reflected on every page of scripture. But that does not indicate that additional male language should be dubbed in by translators when it is not in the original. To a generation conscious of the power of sexual bias in religious language, more accurate translation is a necessity.

This by no means implies eliminating gender from biblical texts when it is present in the original languages. There is nothing gained by a gray neutrality. When sex-specific passages are present, they should be rendered accurately. Real life, after all, has varieties of age, sex, and other distinctions. Frequently the Church has tended to submerge these distinctions as in treating children in worship as if they did not exist until they can think as adults. Yet the fact that children think in less analytical fashion does not mean that they are any less parts of the body of Christ. Indeed, they might be a witness to all to the nature of the reign of God!

II

Language about God simply reflects the concerns which have arisen about language concerning humans. But there is an important difference; humans are finite, God is not. Thus we need to beware of any language that limits God. God is male and female, old and young, helpless as a baby and infinitely powerful. Exclusive use of one kind of terminology for God distorts our image of the Infinite. Yet personal language is necessary to indicate that God is knowable in whatever form God chooses to reveal Godself. We shall deal with the practical possibilities in language about God in pronouns and nouns.

In the English language, unlike some, most pronouns have gender. Thus when one says "he" the image given is male. When a pronoun is used, the reference to the name or noun which it replaces must be clear. Hence "he" refers to a male being. This is not easily avoided. Yet if we wish to use a pronoun for God, we have in the past invariably used "he, him, or his," subtly suggesting that God is male.

There seem to be two alternatives to limiting God in this way to maleness. The first is to alternate male and female pronouns. The second is to avoid pronouns altogether.

Certain problems arise when one adopts the first option. Good English prose demands clarity of reference whenever pronouns are used. When pronouns alternate in gender, clarity rapidly disappears and confusion ensues. Although a commendable balance can be achieved, such usage seems impractical, especially in liturgical texts.

The other option is to avoid using pronouns for God. This can be done much more easily than one might suspect. Indeed, there is a benefit in forcing one to reach for ascriptions of God, the Eternal, the Divine Giver, etc., that pronouns always eliminate. Some would argue that using the name God over and over gets repetitious although we have long done just that with "he." There may be one exception to the elimination of pronouns. A reflexive pronoun is often desirable when one speaks of God's self giving. It is quite possible to use a new term, "Godself," in such instances. Indeed, it has a certain value in expressing the uniqueness of God's own being. Like most neologisms, after a year's use it become perfectly natural just as when we turned from "thou" to "you." Other than Godself, pronouns for God can be eliminated entirely. The same would apply to the use of "she, her, hers" for the Church. The Church is just as male as female and the reference to the "bride of Christ" is simply a metaphor.

The names or nouns for God are much more complex. A vast variety of ascriptions for God is available. One list, published by the Section on Worship of the United Methodist Church, lists over two hundred names for God, many of them biblical. Terms such as "Source of All Life," "Israel's Shield," the "Compassionate One" are but a few. Some terms may be offensive, especially militaristic ones or those specifically male. The possibilities are so great that exploration of them is a valuable theological exercise.

The Bible itself provides far more images for God than those we commonly use. Images of God as the one who gives birth, who nurses, who feeds us are present although overlooked. One has to have experienced a brooding hen to know how apt an image for God such a term is in the Synoptics. Recognition of these female designations for God becomes a new hermeneutical tool in communicating the Biblical message.

Likewise, much of the historical tradition contains references to God in female terms. Theologians as disparate as Chrysostom or Anselm can refer to Jesus as "Mother" or "Sister." Such language comes naturally to some mystics. It is always easier to recognize an existing tradition than to have to create a new one. Sources in bible and history are there although underutilized.

III

The most difficult problems occur in Trinitarian language. At times it is necessary, especially in worship and theology, to make explicit references to the individual members of the Trinity. There also are other terms such as "lord" or "king" which are problematic.

The word "lord" is unique to the English language, not being paralleled in other teutonic languages. Often "lord" is used as the English equivalent of *kyrios* or *dominus*. It comes from an Old English source, *hlafweard*, which became *hlaford*, then "lord." The meaning seems to have been "loaf ward," i.e., "keeper of the bread," a concept found in some modern Scandinavian terms as "meat mother," i.e., "keeper of the food." The word "lady" derives from the Old English *hlaefdige*, kneader of the bread or mistress of the household.

However, the present meaning of words is not necessarily determined by etymology. In feudal usage, "lord" meant a noble person with vassals. The female equivalent was "lady." In the case of the sovereign, the term "lord" could be applied to a monarch of either gender. Thus one of Queen Elizabeth's titles is "Lord of Man," ie., sovereign of the Isle of Man.

One can also argue that "lord" is a substitute for the Hebrew *Adonai* or the Greek *kyrios*, neither of which specify gender. On these bases, a case can be made for using the term "lord" with a reasonable argument that it is not necessarily a male term except in feudal use. Thus the term can be applied both to the first member of the Trinity in prayer ("Lord have mercy") or to Jesus Christ in confessing faith ("Jesus is Lord"). But one must also be prepared to recognize that many people will understand the term "Lord" in a male sense only and that for them it may limit the concept of God by imputing to God only male characteristics. Sometimes one might wish to keep it in Greek as is frequently done in sung liturgy: "*Kyrie eleison.*" But we must live with English and teaching must be done or the term avoided when possible.

The use of the term "king," while equally biblical, is less ambiguous. Again our principle of not rewriting scripture seems best. But when one is writing new materials there are alternatives. In the preface of the United Methodist eucharistic prayer, "King" was changed to "Sovereign." Various other substitutes are possible: "reign" for "kingdom," "ruler" for "king." It does not seem feasible to alternate king and queen. There seem to be sufficient words that cover the concept of kingship without indicating a specific gender.

The greatest difficulty occurs when one has to designate a member of the Trinity. The practice defended here is that in certain instances the use of the terms "Father, Son, and Holy Spirit" is necessary for two reasons; the absence of any acceptable alternatives and the positive desirability of such terms in some cases. But of equal importance is the belief that the number of instances when such use is necessary is quite small. Clarity about the restricted number of these necessary instances can and ought to give incentive for the use of other nomenclature. Only when one is clear about necessary usages does one have security in reaching out for other appellations and freedom to use them. Such knowledge is indeed liberating; the uninformed have no choice but to cling to invariable use of traditional terms.

The term "Son" is less controversial. Undoubtedly Jesus was male since there are only two physical ways to be human. This much remains historical fact. Only a docetic Christology would deprive him of sexual identity. The real point, of course, is that he became human. Thus the term "Son" is of more importance in indicating his humanity than his gender. Some terms that are sometimes substituted, such as "Reedemer" point to a role in Hebrew life specifically male, i.e. that of defending the females of one's family. While the term "Son" may be of offense to some, it need only be used in connection with the other members of the Trinity. "Jesus," "Christ," "Messiah," and a host of alternative terms are readily available.

The Holy Spirit seems less problematic as a name. Some would prefer to refer to the Spirit with female pronouns although this violates the principle of avoiding such use.

The deepest problem of all revolves around use of the term "Father." Some find it impossible to use such a male term; others find it impossible to surrender. We take the position that in certain cases its use is necessary and desirable but that the number of such instances is restricted.

There can be no doubt as to the centrality of the term "Father" in the New Testament witness. Robert Hamerton-Kelly cites Joachim Jeremias: "God is designated 'Father' 170 times by Jesus, and never invoked by another name in Jesus' prayers." "Father" is, perhaps, the most revolutionary term in the New Testament. At a time when devout Jews would not even breathe the name of God lest they profane it, Jesus chose the most intimate and familiar of all human terms available. Such presumptuous intimacy brought on his death: "This made the Jews still more determined to kill him, because he was not only breaking the Sabbath, but, by calling God his own Father, he claimed equality with God." (John 5:18). To give up the term "Father" altogether would be to give up an essential insight of Christianity, the accessibility of God to all. "Father" then is more than just a name, it conveys meaning. Paul suggests that the Spirit works, "enabling us to cry 'Abba! Father!' " (Romans 8:15). The ability to approach God on such an intimate level is part of the essential nature of Christianity.

No other term functions in such a way. The only equivalent is "Mother" which can occasionally be used instead or can be joined: "Our Father and Mother." The term "parent" does not function in this way. No one ever addresses a human person by such a function rather than by name. For many people the term "Mother" will create suspicion or hostility and is open to the same objection as "Father" in restricting the attributes of God to those associated with one gender. Hence "Mother and Father" is probably the most desirable alternative when feasible.

There are, however, seven instances in liturgical texts where the use of the term "Father" seems necessary. That there is only such a small number indicates that we need a major effort to seek other ascriptions in prayer and theological discourse. Such a short list includes passages in which, for theological and ecumenical reasons, unilateral changes are not possible. For example, one cannot alter unilaterally the ecumenical creeds without destroying their special function as testimony to the universal faith of the Church. Other instances derive some of their function from dominical authority and historic usage.

The seven necessary liturgical usages of "Father" are: the address of the eucharistic prayer to the Father in reciting past work of the Father and in invoking others present and future, the doxology at the end of such prayer which summarizes its trinitarian pattern, the similar baptismal prayer over the font in its doxological conclusion, the baptismal formula itself, the Lord's Prayer, and the two ecumenical creeds (Apostles' and Nicene). Since the eucharistic prayer is the Church's most important theological statement, its trinitarian operation is essential and is echoed in the creeds. (A good reason to avoid many so-called "modern" creeds is that they are usually very sexist with regard to human language.) Although the New Testament

Church baptized in other terms, as in the name of Jesus (Acts 2:38), to alter the baptismal formula unilaterally today would be a severe ecumenical blunder. The most powerful expression of prayer known is the first two words of the Lord's Prayer.

Beyond this short list, one has the responsibility of creating and seeking out other ascriptions of God. Such efforts expand our knowledge of and relationship to God.

Occasionally, attempts have been made to substitute other appellations for Father, Son, and Holy Spirit even in the seven instances we have mentioned. Yet these efforts cause even more problems. It should be pointed out that the traditional terms are personal names rather than functional distinctions. The Church, as it hammered out its trinitarian theology over the course of centuries, concluded that the Trinity could not be adequately expressed in terms of mutually-exclusive functions. The doctrine of coinherence states the Trinity's joint involvement in their work. Thus creation is not limited to the First Member of the Trinity as John 1:2-4 makes clear. "Creator" is not a substitute for Father. We have already noted that terms such as "Redeemer" or "Maker" have male connotations that make them inadequate substitutes.

The danger of using only such language as "Creator, Redeemer, and Sustainer" is that ultimately it suggests tritheism rather than trinitarianism. That might be an interesting religion but it is not Christianity. The Christian Trinity is differentiated in person but not in substance or ultimately, in function. One might speak of "First, Second, and Third Members of the Trinity" in theological discourse but that hardly makes good liturgical language.

It may be that at a subsequent time adequate alternatives to "Father, Son, and Holy Spirit" may be found but such terms have not yet been achieved. It took the Church four and a half centuries to define what it meant by "Father, Son, and Holy Spirit." Unless we appreciate the long agony of that effort we are not likely to do better.

Above all, we must learn to be sensitive to the power of words to hurt. Only then will we be concerned to speak justly. But one can change one's patterns of speaking and writing, especially if one has a supportive community to catch one's slips and to encourage one's efforts. Nowhere else is language more intensely communal than in the worshiping Church. Nowhere else can the demand for justice exceed that within the body of Christ.

Female and Male Images of God
in Scripture and Translation
Katharine Doob Sakenfeld

Introductory Explanation

The following seminar was conducted in a participatory style. The material here has been revised to be presented in such a way that the reader can enter into the participatory exercises which were conducted during the seminar.

— — — —

Our title is in some respects perhaps misleading; or we should say it has various complications and possibilities of interpretation. There are two topics which will claim our attention. One is biblical images of God, and the other is the matter of inclusive biblical translation — an issue which is not necessarily specifically limited to the matter of God and images of God, although that is an important part of it. Other issues have been deliberately set aside because they are being covered in other seminars: specifically, the questions of Trinitarian language and of local church strategy.

I. Images of God

Concerning images of God, I think we should take as a starting point an understanding that in the classic view of the church God is understood to be beyond male and female, or neither male nor female, or not being of male gender. Now I am not a church historian or a theologian, and I may not be stating that concern in quite precise terms. But it is certainly possible to find statements in the Church Fathers (and I am using that term advisedly in this case) which indicate that over against paganism, from their point of view, the Church Fathers did not want to say that language such as "God the Father" or "God the Son" meant that God was biologically male. It is important to emphasize this point because I think that it is not at all self-evident to people in the churches. Many people do in fact believe that the church teaches, by the use of the language "Father" and "Son," that God is in fact male — and so discussion of this whole issue can't even begin. From some of the letters which were received in response to the announcements about the National Council of Churches' Inclusive Language Lectionary Project, it is very clear that it is not at all unusual for people to consider God as actually biologically male.

At the same time it is very important to distinguish between a theological doctrine of God, on the one hand, and an experiential understanding of God, on the other hand. The two are not the same. I suggest it is very likely that the Early Church theologians who wrote the theologies which explain very carefully that God is not male did probably, even so, *experience* God as male. I think that distinction is important to keep in mind as we approach the Scriptures. And so, as has been said very well in the Presbyterian document *Language about God: Opening the Door*, language is a "shaper of our reality." And if we talk about God as "Father" and "Son" and "King" and "He" and "He" and "He," then God is *experienced* as male regardless of our official theology or of what other occasional images or language we may bring into use. Despite my own sensitivity to this issue, I know that I still do often hear (experience) the word "God" as a "male" word (in worship or in other settings). Some words are for us culturally gender-specific. "Doctor" is male and "nurse" is female; "chef" is male and "cook" is female; "tailor" is male, "seamstress" is female; and so on. And "God" in that sense functions for most of us much of the time basically as a male word. And that is our starting point. We need to move forward in our use of language, because language not only reflects what has been but can shape what is yet to be. And certainly images are primary shapers of our experience of God and of our theology.

Suppose you were asked to draw a church (imagine your picture for a moment). Most people, even adults, who do this exercise draw a building. Now, suppose you were asked to write a definition of a church. Here adults usually focus on people/God relationships rather than on a building, while young people might still talk about a church building. Now children learn in concreteness and in specifics first, and only later are able to generalize and abstract. So if you say, "don't jump on the couch," and then the child jumps on the couch in the neighbor's house and you say, "But I told you," the child may answer, "No, you told me about the couch in *our* living-room." That ability to generalize or to abstract from a building to a group of people, that kind of conceptual ability, comes only later on in the developmental process of understanding how language works. And so when we say to children — or when we had said to us when we were children — "God is Father" or even "God is like Father," the distinction between image and larger reality (analogous to the distinction between the church building and the community of God) could not readily be made. As that imagery persists and persists without explanation or correction, it shapes the learner's reality more and more strongly.

Here is another exerise that you might try. A group of my students were recently studying the marriage imagery and the family imagery in the prophet Hosea. They were asked by their student leaders to generate vocabulary by free word association in response to various words: husband, king, father, wife, servant, son/daughter. Here are the word lists they turned out from that particular group:

Husband	King	Father	
provider	authority	male	incomplete
intimacy	ruler	some negative feelings	intimacy
authority	majesty	damage	
protector	power	omits	
male	tradition	provider	
	interpersonal distance	security	
	warrior	passive	
	rich	bursts of anger	
	male	quiet strength	
		distance from children	
		encourages independence	
		career expectation	
		understanding	

Wife	Servant	Son/Daughter
female	submissive	child
nurturer	trapped	play
intimacy	powerless	dependent
cook	poor	innocent
submissive	obedient	universal experience
support	neutral gender	potential for growth
follower	personless role	perpetual child
unfocused	subhuman	privileged
provider – family life	nitty gritty	beloved
protective	boredom	irresponsible
bearer of children	unappreciated	mirrors adults near
dependent		heir

Consider the first list which they tossed out, for the word "husband." The first question to consider is, thinking of what you know about marriage in biblical times, how do you think their list stacks up? Are those words suitable for the husband in the marriage role as it was understood in biblical times? There are probably words one might add. Do you think there is anything which necessarily would need to be thrown out from the list that you have been given? There is no right or wrong answer to this; it is a matter of reflection. "Intimacy," for example, is one word about which there might be some question, although there are certainly indications in some Bible stories about relations between husband and wife showing that they genuinely did feel close to and care for one another, even though it may have been the case that marriages were often arranged (we cannot be sure about that).

Now take that same list for "husband" and consider your own understanding of marriage in the twentieth century in our own situation. Now, obviously, you are looking from your own cultural perspective, and there will be considerable diversity among readers. As I said to the students, I would not necessarily expect agreement. Is there anything on the list which creates any feeling of discomfort for you or doesn't quite fit? In the class itself, and in the COCU seminar, each item except "intimacy" was eliminated by at least some group members, but not everyone agreed on which items to eliminate. Clearly there are people in our own culture who feel that it is certainly the husband's role to be the "provider" — whatever exactly they understand to be meant by that term. Obviously there are many people who feel that it is the husband's responsibility to hold authority in the family situation. What about "protector"? There may be many people who would ditch that one intellectually but will still hold on to it very tightly in other kinds of ways in their lives.

The point of the preceding exercise is twofold. First, the image that was working, that was effective, that was commonly understood for Hosea as he worked and spoke to the people in 740 B.C. cannot be counted upon to match the image of marriage which functions for modern hearers/readers of the Bible. Second, and equally important, even if you use a contemporary image, if you talk about what it means to be a husband in our culture, you cannot without explaining yourself have any assurance that the person listening to you is thinking or experiencing the same thing as you are as the speaker in the situation. Images do not communicate univocally; therefore they need to be explored rather than simply presented.

Now, looking again at that same list of words, erase in your mind the heading "husband" and replace it with the word "God," and then reflect on what happens. Which words would you keep or question, if any, if they are applied to God? Again, responses from previous individuals have been varied. Some want to keep "protector" but eliminate "provider"; some want to do the opposite. Again, the key point here is that images are not univocal. When we use images — biblical images or other images — we cannot simply assume that the parts of the image that we have picked up as appropriate to who God is are the same parts of the image that the next person is picking up. So we must begin to spell out, perhaps through this kind of exercise, what it is that we do and don't want to say. This is one way of opening up people, I think, to deal with other kinds of images. You can explore the other lists for yourself in this same way. You might try to create and evaluate a list for the word "mother." Incidentally, the list for the word "servant" is especially fascinating. After you have looked at that list, you might want to reflect on a familiar hymn like "You servants of God." "Trapped, personless, subhuman, bored, unappreciated"? Or, how do people hear the text in Philippians about Christ coming in the form of a servant? Once again, when you ask people about their associations with the word, the responses you get don't fit with the way we are using these images in our religious language. We need to deal with this incongruity.

Against this general background about imagery, we turn to female imagery for God in Scripture. Consider first the New Testament parable found in Luke 15:8ff, about the woman who lost a coin. Here is the RSV text:

> Or what woman, having ten silver coins, if she loses one coin, does not light a lamp and sweep the house and seek diligently until she finds it? And when she has found it, she calls together her friends and neighbors, saying, "Rejoice with me, for I have found the coin which I had lost." Just so, I tell you, there is joy before the angels of God over one sinner who repents.

First of all, notice the Lukan context and the alternation here. This text is preceded by the story of the Good Shepherd and followed by the story of the Prodigal Son. In the Gospel of Luke it seems that Luke tends either to parallel or to alternate illustrations which are especially pertinent to men with those pertinent to the life of women (not necessarily in terms of images of God, but just in general). Now what kind of reaction do people have when hearing this story? Here is a catalogue of some that I have heard:

> "I never noticed that God was portrayed as a woman." (That was my own experience, too.)

> "The only thing that occurred to me in hearing the story was comparing the sinner with the coin as something of value."

> "Well, it was the woman's fault that the coin was lost." (This is a very common reaction. It is not the shepherd's fault that the sheep was lost; it was obviously the dumb sheep that went astray! But here is a woman who lost this coin; after all, women are always losing things.)

Other people have reacted to this story by saying that the woman is a "compulsive cleaner" — which is a very negative image about women. Women are stereotyped negatively as compulsive about their housekeeping. So the idea of the persistent searcher, which is very positive in the shepherd story, disappears as soon as you get to the woman searching for her coin.

If the image of the "persistent searcher" seems remote, then perhaps "housekeeper" would come to mind. Can we picture God as "housekeeper"? The term raises exactly the question which we raised previously. Is the word "housekeeper" a neutral word or a female word (with "cook" as opposed to "chef")? And related to that, why (except that the English pronoun "he" is of course all through our text) — why don't we picture the shepherd as a woman or a girl instead of as a man? In the Old Testament there are very clear examples of women shepherding. The most prominent one is in Genesis 24, where the servant of Abraham comes to get a wife from the home country for Isaac and the first girl he meets is Rebecca, who comes to give her flock a drink of water at the well. Clearly, shepherding would have been a girl's or a woman's responsibility in certain situations. That realization opens up new possibilities for the image. The word "shepherd" is not sex-specific. Likewise, "housekeeper" is not sex-specific. But we have certain associations with both of those words.

Consider the woman and her coin once again. Can you picture God as that searching woman? (Close you eyes if you like.) Can you picture that woman searching by lamplight in the dark dirt of the corners, probably of a dirt-floored one-room house? Or can you picture God — if we want to make it a contemporary image — as a ghetto mother in one of our cities, in one of those dark tenement hallways where the lights never work, whose change for the bus has fallen out when her change purse happened to open while she was hunting for her key? Or to put it in terms of our traditional categories, recall some church sanctuary in which there is a stained-glass window of the Good Shepherd that has meant something to you over the years. Can you imagine in your church a stained-glass window (up in the front, now, not off on the side) of this woman searching for that coin? There are different ways in which images contain power. Picture that woman alongside the Good Shepherd. Or, how about a new banner for your church? (That would be easier than knocking out a wall!) Is there a way in which you could bring this image to life? It can be done. But it takes visual power — more than just words — to get the image across. Whom do you know whose understanding of God might be enriched or changed or challenged by that kind of image?

Now let me call your attention much more briefly to a few Old Testament examples of female imagery for God. First, God is pictured like a midwife in Psalm 22:9 and Psalm 71:6. I would suggest an inclusive translation of the Psalm 71 text:

> Yet you are *the one* who drew me from the womb, who placed me secure at my mother's breast.

Now the RSV translates, "Thou art *he* who drew me from the womb" — and that already gets us into the technical matter of the Hebrew language that belongs in the next section of our study. The Hebrew grammatical form is a participle, and participles in Hebrew have to be either masculine or feminine; there are no neuter forms. This is a masculine participle, so the RSV translates "he who drew me." And of course today (although customs are in flux) we have gone so far with mostly male obstetricians presiding at childbirth that the image of midwife is even harder for us to recapture than it might be for people in another cultural context where midwives are commonly available rather than the exception that we have to go hunting to find. But the image here is clearly a midwife image, a role only for women in Israel. And there is not any pronoun "he" in the text. This is one of the complications of Hebrew grammar — that the grammatical form whenever God is being referred to will consistently be masculine even though the word may be (as we shall see in the next example) "to give birth." So there is a discontinuity between the technicality of the grammar and the content of the image. Since Christian theology does not regard that grammatical technicality as evidence that God is male, then we can surely let go of using the pronoun "he" when we deal with such texts.

Next consider the image of a mother giving birth, Deuteronomy 32:18. Again, here is my translation:

> You were unmindful of the Rock that gave you birth, and you forgot the God who struggled (or writhed) in labor pain with you.

Now the word of the first line which I translated "that gave you birth" is translated "begot" (male activity) in the RSV main text, and in the RSV footnote "who bore you" (female activity). The word in Hebrew is used for either one, and you cannot tell technically which is meant by the form. You have to figure out from the context which one is meant. The word in the second line about labor pain is clearly a word referring to women — except when it refers to God, once again, we have a masculine form of the participle for writing in labor pain. If you compare the RSV or the New English Bible, for example, in the first line you get "to beget" rather than "to give birth" for the Hebrew word which can mean either one. The line is part of a poem, and since God as the subject here is called the Rock, the subject itself does not give us a clear clue about the verbal meaning. If you look to scholars who have done exegesis of this passage, they either take "to beget" and to have labor pains as presenting both a male and a female image of God back-to-back, or else they take both of these as female because of the location of this verse in the overall structure of the poem of Deuteronomy 32, which in a earlier place (v. 6) has a reference to God as Father — a fairly unusual occurrence in the Old Testament. So we have some kind of pairing. In any case Deuteronomy 32:18 is a strong image of Israel's coming into being, with one line which has to be viewed completely as maternal. Because the question of accurate translation constantly comes up, you might be interested to know what the Good News Bible does with this line. Remember that this is considered to be a translation, not a paraphrase.

> They forgot God, their might savior,
>
> [That's from the line, the Rock that begot you, or bore you.]
>
> the one who had given them life.
>
> [That's the one who writhes in labor pains.]

So the range of what can be defined as translation is not as narrow as some purists would perhaps want it to be. But the imagery in a translation such as this Good News Bible one is "explained" to the reader rather than left ambiguous.

In Isaiah 42:14 we find another instance of the birth-pangs imagery. Here is the RSV translation:

> For a long time I have held my peace,

> I have kept still and restrained myself;
>> Now I will cry out like a woman in labor,
>>> I will gasp and pant.

This passage has been described as "the birth-pangs of God." And other texts in the latter part of Isaiah compare God to motherly characteristics: 46:3-4; 49:14-15; 66:13.

One last text deserves special attention. This text is Hosea 11, "Out of Egypt I have called my son." In most of the commentaries it is labeled in large capitals, "The Divine Father" or something similar. We read in the RSV:

> When Israel was a child, I loved him,
>> and out of Egypt I called my son.
>
> The more I called them,
>> the more they went from me;
> they kept sacrificing to the Baals,
>> and burning incense to idols.
>
> Yet it was I who taught Ephraim to walk,
>> I took them up in my arms;
>> but they did not know that I healed them.
>
> I led them with cords of compassion,
>> with the bands of love,
> and I became to them as one
>> who eases the yoke on their jaws,*
>> and I bent down to them and fed them.

*For this very difficult Hebrew line, many other translations read, "who lifts a little child to the cheek."

The first thing to be seen is that this poem is all in the first person. In the first person in Hebrew grammar — unlike the participles — there is no distinction between male and female forms; we cannot say from the grammar that the speaker has to be male or female. So on what basis have scholars traditionally concluded that here we have a divine Father speaking? Because Hosea is using familial imagery? Because he uses the image of God as husband in chapters 1-3? Because God is called Father elsewhere in the Old Testament? The image of chapter 11 is obviously a parent. But think for a moment about what the parent does.

> The more I called them, the more they ran away.
>
> I lifted them up in my arms, I taught them to walk,
>
> I healed them, I held them to my cheek (the suckling child is the Hebrew word here).
>
> I bent down and fed them.

Within Israelite culture, as far as we can know it, surely this is a series of activities that a mother would be likely to do. It has often been my experience that readers of Hosea 11 will conclude that it is a mothering image just as soon as they realize that no father is explicitly mentioned. My own inclination is to argue that this idea can be further supported from the overall purpose of Hosea's message to his own times and people. When Hosea presents God as the divine husband in the opening chapters of the book, part of what he is doing is placing Yahweh over against Baal the fertility god, because

Hosea's basic complaint is that the people are into all kinds of fertility cult apostasy. That is why he uses the harlotry and adultery imagery. But setting Yahweh the God of Israel over against Baal implies also setting Yahweh over against the mother-goddess of fertility who is Baal's wife. This goddess is thought of more as mother than as wife, I suspect, and thus it seems possible to argue that there in chapter 11 Hosea presents indirectly Yahweh as the mother over against the fertility goddess mother figure of the Canaanite religion that he is challenging. Thus the images belong in pairs. It is not simply that you have Israel presented as a wife in chapter 2 and a son in chapter 11 — a female and male image of Israel held in tandem in the two parts of the book. But there may also be specific overtones of saying that Yahweh alone is God by presenting Yahweh as the husband in chapter 2 and as the mother in chapter 11.

Must we determine whether the image of Hosea 11 is one of a father or a mother? Must we choose between them, or can we use "parent"? The question is important, especially for a culture where child care responsibilities are in flux. What are the pros and cons of going to "parent" as a metaphor for God rather than using both "mother" and "father" as we see to be possible from these various biblical texts? The word "parent" is not a word like "housekeeper" or "firefighter," able in theory to be either masculine or feminine but by cultural tradition usually perceived as feminine and masculine respectively. By contrast, "parent" must be able to be either male or female, by definition. So one could argue that "parent" would be the ideal metaphor upon which to focus. But the question of what each of us hears when we use that word still would have to be asked, because for many people the word "parent" can become just a safe excuse for avoiding the image of father while not getting into the experiential issue of who God really is, and never having to think through the concept of God as mother, which most people experience first as incongruous, threatening, and unbiblical. So in God-talk the word "parent" tends to function simply as a substitute for the word "father" — male because that is the only category of the image that is familiar. On (and this is an additional problem) the word "parent" functions as an abstraction. We don't address someone as "parent." We have incorporated such usage into many prayers ("O divine Parent," or something like that), but we don't talk that way in ordinary conversation; we address an individual as either "mother" or "father." And how do we deal with that matter of address, as we use images? Perhaps we should focus on particular activities associated with the image, rather than being limited to the male or female images *per se*. Our seminar topic raises many areas for further reflection.

II. Bible Translation

What is your conception of translation? Already the illustrations in Part I have raised the question. Obviously a translation is not an interlinear Bible. If any of you have tried using a Hebrew interlinear Bible, where the words in the two languages are printed in opposite directions on the page, you will have some feeling for the impossibility of trying to use such a device in any liturgical setting, which is our focus here. But what is the definition of a "literal" translation? Is it fair to say that literal translation means conveying the thought of the text in our own language? That is a possible definition, but it requires two very tricky steps: one is to discover the thought of the text, and the other is the problem of agreed-upon rules of English (for us) usage in language. Part of the reason translation is diffiult to do is that the rules of what is correct English are now very much up in the air in regard to the whole inclusive-language question.

Here is a simple example of how English grammar rules affect translation. There are all kinds of places where the word "it" is used in the Old Testament in English Bibles. But like the Hebrew participles discussed in Part I of our seminar, all words in Hebrew have to be either masculine or feminine; there is not any neuter category. But that grammatical difference does not require the translators to say "she" or "he" for things which we in English regard as neuter (for example, in English rocks are not "she," houses are not "he"). So obviously the standard of what is correct English grammar and speaking and writing controls certain aspects of what we do when we translate. If it were the case that inclusive language were a standard of English grammar, and that you could not say something in a non-inclusive way because non-inclusive forms simply did not exist in acceptable grammatical English (or were so archaic that they could not be understood), then the standards for translation would be much clearer. Now we are in a transition phase. It should be noted that the RSV Committee is working on a new edition which will translate inclusively every human referent which was intended to be inclusive in the original Greek or Hebrew text. Exactly what shape these changes will take is not yet clear. Perhaps, for instance, where we now have "brethren" or "brothers" in Paul's letters, we will have "brothers and sisters" (I do not know the Committee's decision). Some people say "sisters" is not in the Greek text; and "brothers" does not mean "friends," so we can't use "friends" either; we just have to say "brothers." That is the kind of issue at which we are looking. Places where the RSV says, "he who does so-and-so can be saved" can become "the one who . . ." or "whoever . . ." Some singulars may be changed to plurals — "they" and "those." "Men" will become "people" unless the text is obviously referring to men over against women and children. The words for "son" and "child" carry distinct connotation in both Hebrew and Greek as well as in English, so there will be decisions to be made in each case with the word "son." But the use of biblical images for the people of God gives urgency to the translation issue. I was at a church judicatory meeting recently in which a male minister approached a woman minister standing next to me, pointed right at her and said, "You are a son of God." The expression was so incongruous to us when it was put that explicitly; but he did not even notice that he had said anything jarring. Such an experience reveals that literal translation is not always the most faithful rendering of the biblical text or of the intentions of its authors.

Psalm 1 begins, "Blessed is the man who walketh not in the counsel of the ungodly" (King James Version). But the text switches to the plural inclusive when it tells about the opposite side. "The wicked are not so." To change the opening singular to a plural probably does not do great violence to the Hebrew text in such a case. It is again a question of whether a translation must allow a reader to reconstruct the original Hebrew/Greek from the English. I don't think that is a very constructive approach to translation, even generally, and especially not in matters of inclusive language.

Psalm 8 presents another classic problem. The RSV in verses 4-5 reads:

What is man that thou art mindful of him,
    and the son of man that thou dost care for him?

Yet thou hast made him a little less than God . . .

Now, to maintain rigorous fidelity to the intention of the original author of the Psalm, I would translate:

What is a frail mortal [the Hebrew word is *'enosh*] that thou art mindful of him,
    or a member of the human race [that is what a *ben-'adam* is] that thou dost care for him?

But the problem is that this Psalm is the background for the Son of Man tradition in the New Testament. So if we don't keep "the son of man" in Psalm 8:4, how will the English reader know to make the connections with the Son of Man in the interpretation of Jesus? Psalm 8 already had a different nuance in New Testament times from what it meant when it was first written.

So, what is the exegetical standard to be? What is the goal of the translation? What is the person who does not know the original language supposed to be able to find out? You see how complicated the question of making a translational decision becomes. If I were preparing an inclusive langauge lectionary for liturgical use, I think I might change the whole of Psalm 8 to the third person plural. Or one could change it to the first person plural. There are other ways of dealing with it. And again, we must keep asking the question of whether we have violated the sense of the Psalm by making it clear that it applies to the reader, the speaker, the hearer in the liturgical setting.

I have mentioned the work of the RSV Committee. The National Council of Churches of Christ, which sponsors the RSV work, is also sponsoring an "inclusive language lectionary project." The goal is to make an inclusive translation (including God-language) of lectionary passages for liturgical use. Such a project invites all of us to think very carefully about the purposes of different translations. We need to consider, for instance, the difference between a biblical translation which is going to be used in public worship and one which is supposed to be used for study by people who have no, or limited, access to the original languages. I think that we often fall into the trap of making a translation for one purpose, with one set of goals, and then using it in all sorts of other kinds of settings without any specific regard for this kind of question at all. Even the most strict translation of biblical poetry has to be done with some kind of latitude because the thought simply cannot be conveyed exactly by a literal translation. The question then, in translation is, can you let the text say what is says (as opposed to what it said)? Can you do that and still not be accused of letting it say what you want it to? I think that there is space to be able to do that. It is a matter of deciding from which end we are going to start explaining. If in Psalm 8 we decide to translate "man" and "son of man," then we must explain that the words mean a frail mortal and a member of the human race. If we decide to translate "frail mortal" or "one little member of the human race," then we have to go back and explain: "Now in the Hebrew this was a certain phrase which was then picked up and used with another meaning in the intertestamental and New Testament periods." That is another kind of explaining. But either way, we are going to need to explain. For liturgical purposes, we should take seriously the possibility of starting from the inclusive side and explaining from there.

We conclude this seminar by considering the matter of pronouns for God. Imagine (although I think it is very hard for us to get our minds around this) that when English-speaking Christians talked about God they did not use any pronouns. Imagine that this were an English-language convention, a standard usage, so that people talked that way without thinking about it. When they talked about people, they would identify them as "he" or "she," but when they talked about God, they didn't use pronouns. Rather, they used images, metaphors, what might be called circumlocutions by today's English standards: "the one who," "the divine," etc. If that were the convention in English speaking, then it would follow naturally that in Bible translations there would not be any pronouns for God either, because that wouldn't be proper English, that wouldn't be the way we talked or read. Translation is dependent constantly upon our existing standards.

To conclude, I don't think that we will experience or know the meaning of inclusive human language at the deepest level, or really be able to communicate or share that meaning on a wide basis, until our experience of God is somehow different from that of the male deity alone. I mean that statement both psychologically and theologically, speaking of all humankind in the image of God. The time will come, and will come at different points for each of us, when suddenly or gradually we experience the truth rather than the dissonance of a female metaphor for God. That experience may happen through the constant lifting-up of those metaphors, and yet it always comes in a particular context. It often includes the dissonance of a male metaphor for God which has always seemed perfectly adequate in the past. There may be times when we have to silence some of the images which are too painful. There may be a practical intermediate step of lifting up the wide array of images that are not sex-specific. As a final exercise, make a list of images — like shepherd, friend, confidant, teacher — a list of the words which are personal metaphors, vocational-activity metaphors, some of which could be either male or female although we may not usually perceive them as such — images which help you to think about God. Share your list with your friends; keep it over a period of time; compare notes with others and expand your list. Don't let your God be too small.

That Language Issue*

Arlo D. Duba

Where are we on the language issue? How are we dealing with language in our congregations, especially in our worship services?

Some of us got on board ten years ago, and we worked with some diligence trying not to address our parishioners as "brethren." We participated when the women's groups in our denominations raised questions concerning the appropriateness of the exclusively masculine orientation of our God-language.

But many of us have grown fainthearted. I am hearing with disquieting frequency from people who have "given up" on the language issue, pastors who are letting down their guard and going back to old habits of speech. Don't do it! The Church of Jesus Christ moves by its proclamation, by its words. And consider that the imperative of the gospel is laid upon us to watch our language. This is one of the most important tasks we have.

We form our language, and then our language forms us. Language which is first a servant of the Word may become a despot, contorting the Word. And the language we use — especially the language of worship, praise and prayer molds and engraves minds and hearts. Language is our gift to the future. So those of us who are ministers of the Word dare not be cavalier in our use of words.

We know that language is a living thing. Language is constantly changing, and the English language is changing rapidly. Can we change quickly enough to keep up? The latest edition of *Roget's Thesaurus* no longer lists the word "mankind." "Humankind" has replaced it. McGraw-Hill, Macmillan, Scott Foresman, and Houghton Mifflin, names which we associate with the textbooks our children use, for nearly a decade have limited the use of such words as "man," "brother" and "he" to individuals of masculine sexuality. They assume that there is no longer a generic use of such words. There is a generation of elementary, junior high and high school youngsters coming into our churches who assume that when we say *man* or *mankind*, we mean a person or all persons of male sexuality. In that context, the phrase "God calls us to be brothers" excludes half the church.

So while we may assume (and perhaps rightly so) that the issue of inclusive language is of little importance to many of the older people in our churches, it is difficult not to conclude that an attempt to use masculine language as "generic" will be interpreted by children and young people in our congregations as excluding women and girls.

The same basic guidelines operate in the television industry. Thus, the communication industry as a whole is guided by usage that is quickly becoming established both consciously and subliminally. There are both subtle and blatant forces at work which say, "There is no generic use of masculine words, and anyone who uses such outmoded expression will surely be misunderstood." For those of us who believe that communication is one of our primary functions, and who have great concern for the rising generation, this is indeed a sobering thought. To disregard how our children and young people hear us is to be irresponsible.

Does Our Language Defend the Faith?

Throughout the history of the Christian faith, theologians have been careful to emphasize that God is not male and God is not female. God is not of one sex. God is not of both sexes. God is beyond sexuality. For those languages that are grammatically inflected, this understanding causes no difficulty. Grammatical gender has, in the vast majority of cases, no relationship whatsoever to sexuality. In French, to say *la table* does not in any way imply that a table has feminine sexuality or *le salon*, that a living room is connected in any way with masculine sexuality. But in English, to say he, brother, or man does carry the meaning of masculine sexuality to the exclusion of the feminine in exactly the same way that she, sister, or woman carries the implication of female sexuality to the exclusion of the masculine.

Again, given the developing guidelines and style rules for American English, and granting that for children and young people the use of masculine pronouns automatically connotes masculinity, the continued use of *God: he* language flies in the face of the Christian tradition. We could go so far as to say that it encourages idolatry. In other words, it is precisely because we want to retain the historic Judeo-Christian understanding of God that we must change our *God:he* language and find some other. It can be argued that those who are not conscientious enough to do so are aiding and abetting heresy.

The Pastor as Resident Theologian

Those who minister in the local church have the responsibility to know what people are hearing them say, and they have the responsibility to be interpreters. What did the apostle Paul mean when he said, "I would have you know, brethren . . ." (Gal. 1:11) or "I appeal to you, brethren . . ." (Gal. 4:12)? Was he separating out only the males who were among the saints in Galatia? Quite obviously, not. He was speaking of both male and female (Gal. 3:28), of both brothers and sisters. And if that is what he meant, that is what we should say. If our language has now changed to the extent that the use of the "brothers" will exclude half of those whom Paul included, it is our responsibility, in being faithful to what Paul said, to interpret this for our hearers.

In the present linguistic ethos, great care needs to be taken in the reading and proclamation of Scripture. It is now common knowledge that translators in both the 17th and 20th centuries indiscriminately sprinkled generic "men" throughout the Scripture. We need to use the Greek New Testament more, if only to check for that little word *tis*, which simply means one, someone, anyone.

> Faith is God's gift. It is not of works, let anyone (*tis*) should boast (Eph. 2:8-10).
>
> If anyone (*tis*) is in Christ, there is a new creation (II Cor. 5:17)
>
> Behold, I stand at the door and knock. If anyone (*tis*) hears my voice . . . (Rev. 3:20).

Nor should we permit stereotypical interpretations of Scripture to stand. The two disciples on the way to Emmaus could well have been a man and woman, a possibility strongly suggested, inasmuch as it appears that they were going to their home. Of course, we await with eagerness the translations of the Bible that will incorporate the new guidelines, but in the meantime, this ministry of translation and interpretation is one of the pastor's primary theological tasks.

We must affirm, at the same time, the historical nature of the documents of our faith, whether we speak of the Scriptures, hymns, or prayers. There are places where we would now speak differently than earlier writers did. John 1:13 is specific, "not of the will of man (*aner*) but of God," where it seems evident that one should more accurately say, "not of human will but of God's will." But the Greek does not use *anthropos* here as we would expect. Luke is much more careful. In Luke 5:18 ff., some men (*andres*) brought to Jesus a person (*anthropos*) to whom Jesus said, "Person (*anthrope*)! Your sins are forgiven!" Earlier in that chapter the disciples are told that they will catch people, not men or fish (5:10)!

The Problem of Hymns

Hymns provide the most prevalent and most difficult problem. They are works of art that have an artistic integrity which must be respected. Many hymns are sufficiently recent to be covered by copyrights. What can be done in these cases?

It is becoming evident that some hymns must be considered as period pieces and relegated to history. "Once to every man and nation" is such a hymn. Both the imagery and the language are from another era, and use in our time would be ill-advised.

Some hymns can be changed at the expense of the poetry. "In Christ there is no east or west," written by John Oxenham to express human unity, now finds itself excluding all women. The line "close binding all mankind" could be changed to "close binding all the world," but this no longer rhymes with " . . . high communion find." Each pastor-musician team will have to weigh the merits of (1) the message of the hymn, (2) the artistic integrity of the hymn, and (3) the theological-pastoral demand for using language which expresses what should be expressed.

Some hymns will actually be improved by changes. The hymn "At the name of Jesus," for example, has little offense. The stumbling block is the first word of the last stanza where Caroline Nobel wrote, "Brothers, this Lord Jesus . . . ." Much stronger is the substitution of "Surely this Lord Jesus . . ."

Change in the Congregation

How can we effect these changes in the congregation? One of the chief means will be by exercising care in the reading of Scripture and in its proclamation in sermons. With reference to hymns, the preferred method seems to be to indicate the changes in the worship bulletin. A legal opinion has been expressed that whereas it would be illegal to rewrite copyrighted material in its entirety, it is not a violation of copyright to say:

Hymn 143	"At the Name of Jesus"	*King's Weston*

Stanza 4:

please change "Brothers" to "Surely"

Hymn 342	"O God of Bethel"	*Dundee*

Stanzas 2 & 3:

please change "fathers" to "forebears"

Hymn 11	"Holy, Holy, Holy"	*Nicea*

Stanza 3:

please change "sinful man" to "sinfulness"

Changing *God:he* language is not nearly so easy. Some have determined to use the word God as subject and object but occasionally to allow the masculine pronoun to stand as a modifier or in a reflexive position. For example:

Praise the Lord

Praise the Lord! O heavens, adore him
Praise God, angels in the height
Sun and moon, rejoice before him
Praise God, gleaming stars and light
Praise the Lord, for God has spoken
Worlds his mighty voice obeyed
Laws which never shall be broken
For their guidance God has made.

Praise the Lord, for God is gracious
Never shall his promise fail
God has made his saints victorious
Sin and death shall not prevail
Praise the God of our salvation
Hosts on high, God's power proclaim
Heaven and earth and all creation
Laud and magnify God's name.

Another example, which completely removes the masculine references to God:

Praise to the Lord

Praise to the Lord, the Almighty, the God of Creation
My soul, sing praises, for God is your health and salvation
Let all who hear now to God's temple draw near
Joining in glad adoration.

Praise to the Lord, who o'er all things is wondrously reigning
And as on wings of an eagle, uplifting, sustaining
Have you not seen, all that is needful has been
Sent by God's gracious ordaining.

Praise to the Lord, who will prosper your work and defend you
Surely God's goodness and mercy shall daily attend you
Ponder anew what the Almighty can do
If with such love God befriend you.

Praise to the Lord! O let all that is in me adore you
All that has life and breath, come now with praises before you
Let the amen sound from your people again
Gladly, forever adore you.

The changes in these hymns are so extensive that a full text is necessary. If they were under copyright, the provision of such a full text could be copyright violation.

As we await new translations of Scripture, we wait even more eagerly for new hymn texts. New hymns are appearing more and more frequently, but it will still be some time before a whole body of hymnody will be available that meets the new guidelines. In the meantime, valuable collections are appearing, such as *Everflowing Streams*, edited by Ruth C. Duck and Michael G. Bausch, available from Pilgrim Press in New York. This collection provides excellent changes for "A mighty fortress," "All creatures of our God," "All servants of God," "Be thou my vision," "Christ for the world we sing," "For all the saints," "God of grace and God of glory," "Joyful, joyful we adore you," and 30 or 40 others, as well as providing some new hymns. All copyrights have been cleared for these. In this collection even words like "Lord" and "Master" have been altered. For example, "Praise to the Lord, the almighty," used in the example above, appears as "Praise be to God, the almighty."

The Episcopal Church in Hymns II provides 150 new and altered hymns. But even these do not reflect the consistent application of the guidelines and will not be entirely sufficient for the conscientious worship leader in preparing for Sunday worship.

In coming months watch for these names: Ruth Duck, Brian Wren, F. Pratt Green, and Jeffrey Rowthorne, among others, who are writing hymn texts in full awareness of the issues here raised.

Concerns about language are ecumenical concerns. Concerns about hymns are ecumenical concerns. It seems evident that what is needed in the immediate future is an ecumenical consultation which could provide hymn texts on which there is consensus. Whereas hymn texts were once a common bond among us, each denomination or publisher now has provided idiosyncratic textual alterations, and our worship has been fragmented. Both the Consultation on Church Union and the Hymn Society are considering the development of a body of commonly accepted hymn texts, but the task is so immense as to be staggering.

In the meantime, we exercise our pastoral office by taking care in using the hymns we have, we watch for new and altered hymns, and we support efforts toward reestablishment of a body of ecumenical hymnody that adequately reflects contemporary theology and usage.

The Local Church as a Model for Change

Ann Cally Rogers-Witte

Our assignment here in this seminar is to talk about practical, down-to-earth ideas for getting local churches to use more inclusive language. This is not a theological seminar or a theoretical discussion; it is a time to think about very concrete ideas for introducing change into a local congregation. In this session we leave behind the philosophical discussions and face the pragmatic problems. In this seminar we are talking about ways to reach the woman who says, "But I've always thought mankind included everyone" and the man who jokes, "I don't care if you change the words in the Bible, but please don't change the pictures!"

I assume that our goal in this session is to *speak of ways to encourage the use of more inclusive language about persons and about their relationship with God in our local congregations.* I want to share with you ideas and strategies that have worked in my own local church and in churches of other persons whom I know. Then, I want to ask you to enter into the dialogue and share ideas and strategies which you know have worked or which have a good chance of working.

First, let me explain the process I followed in preparing for this seminar. I enlisted the help of my friends! I wrote letters to a number of clergy friends or acquaintances of mine in whose churches I suspected some things might be happening in relation to this issue. In no sense is this a scientific survey; I simply wrote to some folks I know. It happens that most of them are United Church of Christ clergy. Most of the people to whom I wrote were UCC and thus so were most of the responses, although I did write to some folks in other denominations. I asked these persons for practical "how to" suggestions of strategies, with "real-live" illustrations. I asked them what has worked to produce change in language in their setting. What cautions are advised by those who are trying to encourage the use of more inclusive language?

There were some surprises in my little survey. First surprise: it seemed that, at least among my friends, some male clergy found it easier to push the issue of inclusive language than most of the female clergy. Some of these male clergy seemed to have been more intentional than the female clergy in pushing for change. The female clergy frequently reported some hesitancy; they didn't want to be seen as "one-issue people." That bears out my own experience. I don't push it as much as I might. In the congregations which I serve there are surely a number of persons who affirm the use of inclusive language, but many others simply go along with it "because it makes Cally happy and we can surely humor her a little bit." But certainly not all of the male clergy to whom I wrote are being very purposeful about this issue. In fact, my second surprise was that *many* of the male clergy whom I expected to be doing good things in this area either did not respond to my letter or wrote to confess sadly that they really weren't doing very much. Third surprise: the impetus for change seems not to come from the laity. Of course I only wrote to clergy so that says you can't trust what I've just said. But, at least, the clergy report that, by and large, they are the ones who are pushing this issue and that only infrequently is it pushed by laity. There are some notable exceptions and I will mention at least one later.

One of the most helpful responses I received to my survey was from a friend in St. Louis who sent me a copy of a very lengthy and thorough paper on just this topic by Jane Fisher Hoffman. (In fact, if I had discovered this paper sooner, I probably would have encouraged those who planned this conference to invite her instead of me to lead this seminar. I encourage you to write to her for copies of her work.) One of the things which I appreciated in her paper was a delineation of the three possible *styles* of introducing change on the part of clergy.

First, there is the "direct, head-on" style where the pastor hammers away at inclusive language every opportunity he or she has — in the pulpit, in committee meetings, by telling people what words they must use in the hymns, by admonishing those who forget to change their language. This very direct approach is most effective in churches where the pastor is highly respected and well liked. (It surely backfires if the pastor or leader is abrasive!) But what happens when the much loved pastor leaves? Often the congregation slips back into the old ways because the change hasn't become institutionalized and no one else has really taken any steps to insure the changes. And if a domineering pastor leaves, we can surely expect rebellion in the ranks — with the inclusive language going right out the window!

The second style is the extremely subtle approch — which no one even notices! Most of the clergy who responded to my survey indicated that they always use inclusive language in the sermons and prayers which they personally write, but they wonder if anyone even knows the difference. And one clergy couple wrote me that they thought that the language changes had been owned by their entire congregation but when they came back from vacation one summer, they discovered that the congregation had quit using the booklet with new words to hymns which the couple had prepared and were singing from the old hymnal as if they had never even realized there was a difference! This style — of subtle changes — probably does not lead to lasting change either.

The third style includes the subtle approach just mentioned; obviously the pastor uses inclusive language in his or her prayers, sermons, and in ordinary conversation. But in this case, she or he is much more "up-front" about it — not coercive, but "up-front." The pastor or other leader is careful to *model* the use of inclusive language — but not to stop with the modeling. She or he goes on to say out loud why he or she is using inclusive terms and why that is important, in a fairly gentle but strong way, not forcing anyone else to do the same thing. Several persons who wrote to me suggested strategies for this approach to change. One said, start with the committee which is responsible for worship. Seek their support; engage them in a careful study of the issues. Another said, it is important to listen with care to people's fears, hostilities, and concerns. Be prepared to deal with anger and confusion. We are suggesting some deep-rooted changes. Another suggested that, rather than pushing the church to make official *policy* about language, it is good to encourage the church's *practice* to use inclusive language. For example, this pastor said that their church had not pushed for a formal vote on language, but as a strategy, had begun to use revised language in the liturgy with a note in the Sunday bulletin that this was a trial experiment and if anyone had comments they could tell the appropriate committee. The pastor noted that after several months of very few comments they just dropped the note in the bulletin.

Several respondents said that a "sense of humor" is a necessity in introducing these changes into a local church. And others said that we need to acknowledge the serious difficulties raised by the various questions concerning this issue. One approach that I particularly like was to say to the congregation, "Some of our sisters and brothers, especially some of our sisters, have said to us that they feel left out by the language we use in worship. They are asking us to consider the language we use, to use some news ways of saying things, ways that expand and do not limit. We are going to try some of these ways for a while."

What are some of the most frequent "blocks" to change? What are the responses that people give when faced with change? Some people simply think the whole thing is not very important. "Where there are so many starving people in the world, how can we waste so much time on unimportant language discussions?" Others, often female, say, as I noted earlier, that they do not feel excluded by "generic" masculine terms. They say they've always known that "man" means all humankind. This is a very complex matter; many articles have been written on this subject alone. But surely we need to point out how this "masculine normative" assumption devalues women. At least we can think of the children — they think too concretely to understand that females are included in the generic male term. Then there are the folks — and most of them are like me and have had a loving relationship with their own earthly father — the folks who say, "But 'God the Father' has always meant so much to me!"

Personally I think the key to that comment and the key to the whole thing is to affirm the *multiplicity* of ways of talking about God. Surely everyone can understand that no one human concept can say all there is to say about God! Another block to change is the idea that it's okay to change new things, but "let's don't mess with the old — that's 'history,' that's 'tradition.'" There is some merit to that argument, I think, as to many of the others. But we can use alternate versions of hymns, prayers, and creeds *some* of the time, at the least.

I really do believe that "multiplicity" is the key! People know, deep down inside their being, that we can't box God in with one or two terms. God is broader than any name we would choose. Yes, Father may be a very meaningful title, it certainly is very historic and is traced right back to Jesus, but there are also many other titles for God which can enrich our relationship with God and our understanding about God.

So, that moves us on into the next topic for our consideration: concrete proposals for changing language in *liturgy*, and then for changing language in *congregational life*.

First, liturgy. Most of the replies to my survey were directed to changes in liturgical language, as indeed is this consultation. As I said, most respondents said that they use inclusive language in the sermons, prayers, and litanies which they themselves compose and print in the bulletin. And many folks are pleading for more printed resources; they want more published material with high quality poetic and theological worship aids — prayers, Calls to Worship, Prayers of Confession, credal statements, benedictions. They don't want to have to invent it all afresh each Sunday, and somehow just changing a word here or there in the old resources isn't very helpful. My UCC respondents were highly appreciative of the little booklet, "Worship: Inclusive Language Resources" published several years ago by the UCC Office for

Church Life and Leadership and of the very recent "Bread for the Journey" published by the Board for Homeland Ministries of the UCC. I'm sure there are similar resources from the other denominations, but UCC folks don't know about them. One task for our ecumenical mission is to make existing resources known to everyone! And the other task for all the various agencies is to publish more high quality material.

At this time I would like to read to you some of the selected portions of a few of the letters I received in response to my inquiry. The first one I will read in some detail because it seems like a classical "case study": The pastor writes:

We are a church associated with both a university and a seminary. No formal associations with either, but many members of the congregation are from both. We started an intentional program of inclusive language when I came seven years ago — at the request of several of the seminary persons who worked at raising everyone's consciousness, beginning with mine. This prompted me to make some passing references to the issue in sermons and liturgy, while changing some words, thereby beginning to call attention to the issue, but not to talk a lot about it or ask for policy deliberations. In due time we have done the following: We use inclusive versions of all hymns. (I write the revisions with the help of my rhyming dictionary. We print the revisions in the mimeographed Sunday order of worship. At first I printed them on an insert; now I print them in the body of the page, right under the hymn entry.) We use the inclusive versions of the Doxology and the Gloria. We revised the UCC Statement of Faith and our own church covenant, after some interesting sessions of the Diaconate.

Occasionally now, but not always, we indicate this church's practice (not official policy, we've never asked that question) of using inclusive language. I try not to use more than one revised hymn per Sunday, although I may add another which needs only a line or two for instruction. We've been lucky in several respects: We've had ordination services of women in this church, and several of those women have taken leading roles in the congregation, both before and after ordination. When I was on Sabbatical the first half of this year, a woman seminary senior was chosen as interim minister; she did an excellent job, winning over some of the pockets of male resistance in the congregation . .

It comes to my attention that there are persons in the congregation who continue to sing the old hymns and liturgy. So what? We offer a choice. Since returning from Sabbatical, I observe that when we do a psalter responsive reading, the congregation changes the pronouns in their parts as they go along, just as I change them ad hoc in my parts of the reading. Some phrases change more easily than others, but we ignore a certain amount of stumbling at those points. I sometimes wonder what a newcomer thinks about the whole business of language, since we seldom refer, now, to our practice of revising. Of course we try to deal with other women's issues as well, not just revised language. . . .

That letter reflected the most careful and complete change that was reported to me in my survey. I suspect that pastors of churches *not* connected with a university and a seminary where women students are raising the issue would not find complete change quite so simple. In fact, their comments to me in their letters indicate that that is the case. One female pastor of a blue-collar congregation reports:

> I rarely ask people to sing from the hymnal and make changes. They resent that. I retype the new words on an insert. That seems to be much more palatable. I never refer to "Mother-Father God" — that galls people, too. I use first one such image in its entirety, and then the other. I use "Parent" on occasion. I am "gentle" with people about God-language — and respect their imagery and the theology reflected in their choice of words, but I am tough on inclusive people language.

Regarding possible changes of language in scripture one pastor in Texas wrote:

> Among those discussing the flap that has grown up around the Revised Standard Version texts and their changes, people here wonder why the big deal. I make a practice of suggesting alternative translations to passages in worship and study anyhow. Thus, from an early time in the business of utilizing more inclusive ways to say what is being said, I have felt quite free to liberate a text where that is needed. Sometimes that's been done by using my own translation entirely, but most often I defer with a few adaptations to the major translations that we have for our use.

Another pastor, this time from Tennessee, sent me a number of specific comments. He noted that it was important to him that the word for "Spirit" in the Hebrew and Greek is usually neuter or feminine. He also suggested that Jesus used two methods in his prayers to avoid using God's name lightly and that these two methods might work for us, too: the use of the euphemism "Heaven" (a neuter word) for God, and the use of the passive voice. For example: instead of "let us thank God for His gift of forgiveness," use "Let us be grateful for Heaven's gift of forgiveness." And, another example, instead of "Let us pray that God may inspire us and that (He) may lead us," one might pray, "Let us pray that we may be inspired and led." This same person noted that the change from "Thee and Thou" to "You" was only the correction of an English idiosyncrasy. But the last decade's explosion of awareness of the inclusive langue issue is a true sea change in the Church's life. It will one day be seen as an irrevocable step forward in the Christian faith — implicit but not explicit in the original Gospel — like our current opposition to slavery. It is really exciting to be alive at such a time.

There were also many specific suggestions about hymns. Instead of just changing a word or phrase here or there in a hymn, many people suggested entirely new words to old tunes. That way the congregation can have the familiar old tune, but will pay attention to a new message. Others reported success with introducing new words *and* new tunes. One person was pleased with using an overhead projector during worship to suggest changes in the wording of hymns. A friend of mine counted all the hymns in the *Pilgrim Hymnal* and said that of the 500 hymns, 400 speak of God as He, King, Father, Master, and other masculine terms. 100 speak of God as Redeemer, Judge, Creator, and other non-sexist terms. She looked at a number of other hymnals, too, and didn't find much difference.

The biggest question seems to be related to language about Jesus Christ. Many persons who advocate changing language about persons and about God do not know what to do about the term "Lord," in particular. "Lord" is especially difficult because it is frequently impossible to know whether "Lord" is meant to refer to Jesus or to God. Some people try to avoid using "Lord" to refer to God, but are comfortable using "Lord" to refer to Christ. Others admit the maleness of Jesus as a human person but question whether Christ our Savior is restricted to maleness.

Again, it seems to me, the key is multiplicity. "Lord" is a very key word in our liturgy and our credal affirmations but it does not have to be used to the exclusion of such important titles as "Savior," "Redeemer," "Sustainer," even "Ruler."

The issue of changing the language in scripture is the most problematic for the persons in my survey. Practice varies greatly. Some persons say that they frequently modify the text, except on "old favorites" where everyone would notice. Others say that they never change the language when reading from the Bible on the lectern, but suggest changes in the body of the sermon. In the congregation which I serve we usually have a lay reader who reads from the Bible on the lectern and rarely changes the language. Then I make changes and suggest alternate terminology during my sermon.

Many people noted the importance of having female leadership in worship, and people frequently noted that the congregation's openness to change seemed related to the amount of participation of a "competent" female worship leader, from time to time.

Well, that's enough pump priming related to liturgy. Let me note some things related to congregational life. One pastor noted:

> Here at our church we attacked the "official" statements of the church first in terms of "cleansing" the constitution and some other documents of the old ways of saying things. The only one that caused a bit of heat was the use of "forebears" instead of "forefathers." Strange! Then we noted that the pictures in our historic chapel are of the "heads" of the households —all *men*. We then sought pictures of women other than the pictures of "womanly groupings." That worked, too.

I want to spend a bit more time reading from a response of a lay woman in a church in northern California who sent me a report of their committee which studied constitution and bylaw changes for inclusive language in 1976. She first notes the "context" in which this study took place:

> When our former minister was here he would say, "I disagree with you, but I still care for you," from the pulpit and he would act out that caring, so the statement was a reality. And for 15 years, this congregation has been willing to "try on" new ideas in worship, especially in the summer and at our mid-week worship services. For 20 years our Annual Meetings of the congregation have been times when people speak out — their concerns, their frustrations, as well as their joys. Often we have intentionally programmed Annual Meetings to allow that. And, several years prior to the bylaws study, the woman who chaired that bylaws committee had been our moderator and during her term the Church Council adopted a policy of listening to all concerns/requests —really listening, not just a quick brush off.

That's the context, then, for that one-year study which the congregation did in 1976. She sent a copy of the committee's report of the study and I think it is worth at least highlighting as a case study model for change in language in congregational life.

Here are some quotes from the report:

"The concern of this congregation with the subject of inclusive language began about a year ago when a bylaws committee recommended to the membership that the bylaws be reworded to make the language non-sexist. Specifically it was recommended that the word *chairperson* be substituted for the word *chairman* wherever it appeared.

The reaction was immediate. The word 'chairperson' elicited strong opposition. An alternate suggestion of 'chair' brought forth equally strong objections. The basic issue was recognized, however. Although the 'anti-Chairperson' members could easily have outvoted the pro faction, they voted instead to table the matter for a year, and to study and discuss the issue in the intervening time.

A committee was appointed to develop a process for effective consideration of the issue. An effort was made to appoint a cross-section of the membership in age, sex, viewpoint, etc. The committee finally was composed of 16 such members. After seven meetings a satisfactory process for presenting the issue to the church membership was developed. It soon became obvious that the issue could not be isolated in the framework of the bylaws. There was also the matter of the wording of hymns. The charge to the committee was then expanded to a consideration of inclusive versus exclusive language in the life of the church. The next two committee meetings were devoted to expression of 1) all possible reasons for keeping traditional language, and 2) all possible reasons for changing language so that it would be inclusive. (Several other meetings followed.)

By April the committee was able to recommend the following plans to the council:

1) Resource materials for general use collected and made available in the church library;

2) A meeting co-sponsored by the language committee and the Adult Education group to be held at the end of April to start our all member dialogue. (Two speakers were obtained for this meeting — a man and a woman, both very interested in the issue, who could bring outside moderate viewpoints and some objectivity to our discussions.);

3) A request that during the month of May all boards and committees discuss inclusive language as it pertains to their work in the church (members of the committee were available to attend those meetings, if asked);

4) An evening church council meeting to be held in early June to be devoted to summaries of the discussions of boards and committees and to hearing individuals who wished to present their views for consideration.

Various options were to be considered. All those plans were approved and carried out. The Committee prepared a statement which gave some background for discussion, resource material, the focal points of arguments for and against the use of inclusive language, and possible options to stimulate discussion in the boards and committees.

Following the church council meeting a subcommittee met to formulate recommendations for future action. Their work resulted in formal statement with a preamble which went like this:

> "Believing that God calls us through Jesus Christ to love one another fully and to participate with God and Christ in human liberation, and wishing to enable this church's continuing efforts and response to this call which is currently seen as the equality of women and men in our society and in the sight of God, the wholeness of persons and the wholeness of God, and the use of language which will reflect this, we recommend to the council that . . .   Then followed a list of things like adopting changes in the bylaw language on a trial basis for six months, and calling for evaluation at the end of the year, etc. The statement went on to declare:
>
> 'The members of this church are aware of the feelings engendered by sexist language. We respect those who feel that such language is exclusive, but we also recognize that many of our members consider traditional language to be inclusive. In loving acceptance of each other's views, we therefore acknowledge that some music, prayers, scripture, and other literature cannot be changed satisfactorily, and state that their use does not imply our indifference to the status of women; we also state our intention to introduce those new hymns, prayers, and other materials which have been carefully selected with regard to language.' "

I am impressed by that careful and "caring process!" Surely no one in that congregation will be unaware of the issues. That's a far cry from the pastor who just quietly models inclusive language, hoping that somehow it will "rub off" on folks who haven't even noticed. Some five years after that process, my friend wrote to me: "The bylaws were the 'easy' part! Music seems to be the 'hardest' part. We are still struggling, and our Sunday morning liturgy continues to reflect our struggle."

Well, I could say more. We could talk about the issues raised in our Christian Education programs — the language of curricula, even the stereotypical stories and pictures in the Sunday School books. We could talk about which jobs in the church are reserved for which sex. All of those things relate directly to the issue of language. We could talk about study groups which would search the scriptures for feminine images of and references to God. We could encourage the study of Jungian psychology in our churches, with discussion of what is masculine and what is feminine in each of us. I could tell you the story of the church that has a logo on its stationary with men and women holding hands in a circle — someone was distressed that a man was on top of the circle, until someone else noted that that also meant a man was on the bottom! But I think I will stop here, pass out a very brief list of resources, and then ask you to quietly and individually reflect on a set of questions I have prepared.

Consultation on Language and Liturgy

Discussion Questions:

1. List comments and questions about presentation.
2. Suggest additional ideas to encourage change (especially in "Prayer Book" churches).
3. Suggest concrete ways to change the "blocks" into forces for change.
4. List ideas of what the churches might expect in the way of help from denominational and ecumenical agencies.
5. List additional resources.

AN AFTER WORD

One of the opportunities for blessing and renewal in a conversation toward church union is the necessity for all parties to listen and speak very carefully. Words are important, for they are interpreters of the past and carriers of hope for the future. By their use we can come to share a common vision.

But words are also employed, intentionally or not, to communicate attitudes of condescension and superiority. Christians have become particularly aware of such misuses of language in relationships between races, sexes, and persons with and without (obvious) disabilities.

As nearly as we can tell, Jesus' words to and treatment of, the "little ones" around him always accorded them dignity and respect. This trait of his was *certainly* true in his attitude toward women.

But the language in which the tradition of and about Jesus (and his relationship to God) passed through the ages did not faithfully preserve his own attitude. The language of the Church became masculine-oriented and dominated. Only in recent times have we been reminded that a corrective is possible and necessary if the faith and the Church are to be truly catholic.

This is not simply a matter of justice, although justice is certainly involved in it. It is also a theological question, a question of the catholicity of the Church in a divided world, of what being "one in Christ" means, of how the Holy Spirit can bring us truth and new light as we live in the Church. It is also a question that more and more divides the body of Christ.

Since 1976, when it published an "Alert" on sexism, the Consultation on Church Union has been committed to confronting this question and dealing with it, both theologically and practically. Only by so doing can a uniting church hope to be truly renewed. Central to the existence and growth of male imagery in theology has been the use of language. What is the relation of words to the Word? Crucial questions are at stake here. To give just one example: What language is to be used in addressing God and speaking about God that both enriches the relationship of *all* of us to God, and is harmonious with the inter-relationship of the persons of the Trinity which the Church elaborated in the Councils of the early centuries?

The Consultation on Church Union convened a conference in late 1981 to begin wrestling with such questions in an *ecumenical* way. The ecumenical nature of this meeting was vital. Too long have we tried to deal with such questions in isolated denominational settings. In the Nashville consultation we attempted to open up some of the many dimensions of the question: theological, liturgical, educational (church school and seminary), and musical.

The addresses, seminar lectures, and sermon reproduced here open various considerations in the use/misuse of masculine-language in the churches. They deal with a wide spectrum, from highly technical questions of gender to "how-to" suggestions for the local church wishing to change the perceptions of its people.

I wish to express particular thanks to the two groups responsible for planning the consultation: the Women's Task Force and the Commission on Worship of the Consultation on Church Union. The work of several individuals was also crucial in bringing it and this publication into being: the Rev. John E. Brandon, who did much to staff the meeting, Mrs. Janet Penfield, who chairs the Women's Task Force, the Rev. Jeanne A. Powers, who moderated the planning committee, and Dr. William D. Watley, who is editing this book.

The discussion has only begun. It needs to be carried on throughout the entire Church; all members of the body of Christ, men as well as women, stand to be enriched in this debate. The Consultation on Church Union offers this modest contribution to the discussion as it attempts to envision life in the body of Christ in which all may be truly one and in which each may make a full contribution.

Gerald F. Moede
General Secretary